HANGED
Execution in the Top End

DEREK PUGH
With a Foreword by
Chief Justice Michael Grant AO

Dr. Derek Pugh OAM: Author
HANGED: Execution in the Top End
First published 2026. Text ©Derek Pugh 2026
Original Photographs ©Derek Pugh 2025, unless otherwise attributed.

ISBN: 9781763667150
All rights reserved. No part of this publication may be reproduced, stored in a retrieval system, or transmitted in any form by any means, electronic, mechanical, photocopying, recording, or otherwise, without the prior written permission of the author.
Indigenous Australians are advised that this text includes the names and photographs of people who have passed away.

Design and layout by Mikaela Pugh: mikaelaapughh@gmail.com
Copywriter: Harold Pugh: hsundarapugh@gmail.com

Subjects:
    True Crime.
    Judicial Executions in the Northern Territory.
    Palmerston, Darwin, Northern Territory.
    Australian Aborigines.
    Chinese people in North Australia.
    Pioneers: Northern Territory–social conditions.
    Capital punishment.

Contact: derekpugh1@gmail.com
www.derekpugh.com.au

A catalogue record for this book is available from the National Library of Australia

Acknowledgements

I was thrilled when Chief Justice Michael Grant agreed to write a foreword for this book. His predecessor of seven decades ago, Justice Kriewaldt, was the last judge to award the death penalty in the Northern Territory, and it is heartening to read the opinions of the current chief justice. Sometimes history does not repeat itself, after all.

Thanks also go to my critical friend and proofreaders, especially Peter Whelan for his editing and feedback on the manuscript. Also, to the Library and Archives of the Northern Territory staff and those in the Australian Archives who provided help and support in retrieving information. And once again, thanks to the Northern Territory Department of People, Sport and Culture for the history grant that helped fund the research and produce this book.

Thanks to Wayne Parslow of *Danisam* (www.danisam.com.au) for his time and the use of his ground penetrating radar looking for the possible graves of Koci and Novotny. We were supervised by Museum and Art Gallery of the NT (MAGNT) and thanks go to Jared Archibald, Curator of Territory History.

This is a history of people in the Northern Territory. Indigenous readers are warned that it necessarily names Indigenous people who have died, some of whom under terrible circumstances. While every care has been taken to avoid mistakes in truth, or the repetition of mistruths, some families might still feel pain in the recall of events of the past.

History research in recent years has changed dramatically. I spent only a few hours viewing those awful microfiche images of old newspapers, but many, many hours reading them on National Library of Australia's *Trove*. Trove is gold. It is an online resource from the National Library that functions like a search engine for Australian history, providing access to a vast range of digitised content such as newspapers, books, photographs and maps. Long may it be supported.

Abbreviations of Note:
   LANT: Library and Archives of the Northern Territory
   NAA: National Archives of Australia
   NTTGG: Northern Territory Times and Government Gazette

Contents

Acknowledgements	iii
Timeline	ix
Foreword	xi
Preface: A Hanging Carnival	xvii
Chapter 1: Charlie Flannigan, 1893	1
The Victim	2
Auvergne Station	5
Halls Creek	7
The Police Court	11
The Circuit Court	14
The Gallows	15
Chapter 2: Wandy Wandy, 1893	21
The Victims	22
The Police Court	26
The Circuit Court	27
The Gallows	30
Chapter 3: Moolooloorun, 1895	33
The Victims	34
The Killers	38
The Circuit Court	40
Crescent Lagoon	43
The Gallows	45
Chapter 4: Chung Yeung and Lem Kai, 1899	47
The victim	47
The Circuit Court	50
The Gallows	51
Chapter 5: Jimmy, 1901	55

The Victims	55
The Killers	59
The Police Court	61
The Circuit Court	63
The Verdict	64
The Execution	65
Chapter 6: Alligator River Tommy, 1905	**69**
The Victims	69
The Killer	70
The Trial	72
The Execution	74
Chapter 7: Koppio, 1913	**77**
The Victims	77
Escape	83
Koppio's Trial	84
Debate about the location for the hanging.	85
The Execution	87
Katterinyan's Trial	89
Chapter 8: Jaroslav Koci and Jan Novotny, 1952	**97**
The Victim	97
Grantham's Funeral	100
The Killers	101
The Trial	108
The Verdict	112
NT Administrator approval.	113
Appeal for commutation	115
Direction from the Governor-General	117
A transfer to South Australia?	117
Report from the Crown Law Office	119
The Execution	124
The Cost	125
The Revelation	126
The Infirmary	127
Chapter 9: The Science of Execution	**131**
Efficiency and Method in Historical Executions	136

Chapter 10: Epilogue	139
Fannie Bay Gaol as a Museum	145
Appendix: The List of Murder Trials 1884-1913	149
Bibliography	155
Index	159

Timeline

15 July 1893	Charlie Flannigan is hanged in Fannie Bay Gaol for the murder of Samuel Croker.
25 July 1893	Wandy Wandy is hanged at Malay Bay for his part in the murder of six Malay trepangers.
17 January 1895	Moolooloorun is hanged at Mole Hill (Crescent Lagoon) near the Roper River, for the murder of an unnamed Chinese man.
10 August 1899	Chung Yeung and Lem Kai are hanged in Fannie Bay Gaol for the murder and "cooking" of Chee Hang at Yam Creek.
8 April 1901	Jimmy is hanged at Shaws Creek for the murder of John Larson.
21 December 1905	Alligator River Tommy is hanged in Fannie Bay Gaol for the murders of Henry Edwards, Richard Frost and Nowra.
1 January 1911	The Commonwealth Government takes over the management of the Northern Territory from South Australia.
15 July 1915	Koppio is hanged in Fannie Bay Gaol for the murders of Ching Loy and Lo Sin near the Old Howley Mine.
1922	Queensland abolishes the death penalty.
8 August 1952	Jaroslav Koci and Jan Novotny are hanged in Fannie Bay Gaol for the murder of George Thomas Grantham.
1955	New South Wales abolishes the death penalty for murder (and for all crimes in 1985).

3 February 1967	Ronald Ryan is hanged in Pentridge Prison, Melbourne. He is the last person legally hanged in Australia. He had killed a prison guard during an attempt to escape.
1968	Tasmania abolishes the death penalty.
1973	The Northern Territory Legislative Council passes the *Criminal Law Consolidation Ordinance 1973* which removes the death penalty for the offence of murder in the Northern Territory.
1975	Victoria abolishes the death penalty.
1976	South Australia abolishes the death penalty.
1983	The Australian Capital Territory abolishes the death penalty through the *Crimes (Amendment) Ordinance 1983*. The ACT remains the only Australian jurisdiction never to have carried out an execution.
1984	Western Australia abolishes the death penalty.
1985	New South Wales abolishes the death penalty.

Foreword

Hon Michael Grant AO
Chief Justice of the Supreme
Court of the Northern Territory

A community's attitude to the death penalty provides one of the keenest barometers of its sociological evolution. In Australia, Commonwealth legislation enacted in 2010 blocks any state or territory from reintroducing capital punishment. That reflects a national consensus, at least at the political level, that the death penalty is both inhumane and ineffective as a sentencing tool. That a legislative prohibition is considered necessary also recognises the fact that the death penalty has only relatively recently been altogether abolished in this country, and that public sentiment on the issue is by no means uniform. New South Wales did not abolish the death penalty entirely until 1985, and surveys consistently show that a very substantial proportion of the Australian populace continues to support capital punishment in at least some circumstances. The greatest of the many virtues and values of Derek Pugh's book on the history of execution in the Top End of the Northern Territory is that it reminds us of the past so we are not condemned to repeat it.

The imposition of death as a sovereign punishment has been a feature of human society since time immemorial. It is recorded as early as the 18th century BC and has manifested in every period and culture since that time. Although some modern commentators characterise the death penalty as an artefact of slavery and colonialism, it was also an established feature of monocultural societies and unitary systems. The Athenian legislator Draco was no doubt well-intentioned when he replaced the ancient system of blood feud with a written criminal code. Although only his laws about homicide have been preserved, secondary sources record that the death penalty was the punishment prescribed for most of the offences created under Draco's code, including minor offences such as petty theft. Slavery was the soft option for those few crimes which did not attract capital punishment. The contemporary use of the adjective "draconian" to describe any law with harsh operation hardly does justice to the source material.

Capital punishment formed part of successive legal systems in England from ancient times. Under the common law, the death penalty was applied to a range of offences in addition to murder, including treason, rape, arson, buggery, sodomy and, perhaps most disturbingly, heresy. Henry VIII was its most enthusiastic practitioner, and it is estimated that 72,000 people were executed during his reign, most of them for theft. A death sentence could be commuted for various reasons by a Cabinet comprised of senior government ministers, but that was rarely done for more serious offences. The death penalty for offences such as theft, counterfeiting and forgery was eventually abolished in 1832, no doubt in recognition of the fact that capital punishment for crimes of that nature was draconian in the true sense of the word. By 1861, the only crimes in the English legal system which continued to attract the death penalty were murder, treason, espionage, piracy and arson in the Royal dockyards. However, executions continued to be conducted in public and had for centuries been an enduring source of public spectacle, revelry and morbid attraction.

The English criminal law was brought to Australia with the creation of the penal colony of New South Wales, including the death penalty for stipulated offences together with a power of commutation in certain circumstances. However, the death penalty remained mandatory for murder and treason. When the colony of New South Wales was first proclaimed in 1788 it included the entirety of what is now Queensland and most of the Northern Territory. The area which is now the Northern Territory remained part of New South Wales until 1863, when it was annexed to the colony of South Australia. The main purpose of that annexation was to give South Australia access to more pastoral land; but the new addition was always known as the Northern Territory and was never fully integrated into South Australia in the public consciousness of either place. There was at that time in South Australia a nascent popular feeling against capital punishment, but one which only went so far. Five years earlier the South Australian legislature had abolished public executions generally, but the colony continued to permit public executions of capitally convicted Aboriginal people at the scene of their crime. That differential treatment of Aboriginal offenders also became part of the Northern Territory legal and governmental framework, and is one of the peculiar practices which features in Dr Pugh's history.

By the time of the first execution in the Northern Territory in July 1893, the only two capital offences on the South Australian statute books were murder and piracy with intent to kill. Those same laws had application in the Northern Territory. Following the transfer of the Northern Territory to Commonwealth control in 1911, the general criminal law of the Northern Territory continued to be governed by the *Criminal Law Consolidation Ordinance*, which was originally a piece of South Australian legislation which carried over as a Northern Territory ordinance. Dr Pugh's treatment illustrates that capital punishment and the power of commutation operated with apparently partial effect in the Northern Territory context. As the author notes, of the 10 people who were hanged in the history of the Northern Territory, six were Aboriginal, two were Chinese and two were recent immigrants from the former Czechoslovakia. Of those, seven were hanged in gaol and three were taken out to the scene of the crime in accordance with the view that such a practice was the only way to ensure that the punishment operated as a general deterrent to members of the Aboriginal communities concerned.

Dr Pugh has created a series of vivid tableaux by drawing on contemporaneous sources which describe the crimes, the trials and the executions themselves. Those descriptions are enhanced by the fact that Dr Pugh is a field historian in the old tradition who travels to the sites about which he is writing wherever possible. He brings his historical knowledge directly to the location of an event, and that location in turn informs and enriches his description of the event. The diligence of his research is also apparent from the fact that he has identified and described these 10 executions in circumstances where national background papers written as recently as 2005 identify only the executions of Koppio in 1913 and Koci and Novotny in 1952. Dr Pugh has identified a further seven executions taking place between 1893 and 1905. He is to be commended for supplementing the public record in that respect.

I have personally observed Dr Pugh's dogged research in his quest to locate the death warrants for Koci and Novotny which were issued by the Supreme Court in 1952. He had identified a communication from a Crown law officer by the name of Edmunds which was written on 7 August 1952 and which recorded that the death certificates were:

> "… ultimately endorsed in the margin by the Sheriff and returned to the Judge of the Supreme Court. It is customary for the seal of the Court to be in black wax and for black ribbon to be used."

At Dr Pugh's urging we were able to identify that the files for Novotny and Koci had been kept in the Sheriff's office up until 2003. The Sheriff who was in office at that time had retrieved the files from the court archives because of their historical significance. He recalled that copies of the warrants of execution signed by Justice Kriewaldt were on that file, without the black wax or ribbon which would have adorned the originals. The presumption is that the originals were kept at the gaol to confer the necessary authority on the executioner.

Foreword

The files were unfortunately moved from the Sheriff's office to an unknown location at some time between 2003 and 2015. The search for them continues.

For reasons that this book makes plain, the appetite of the Northern Territory community for capital punishment diminished over the years. That was reflected in a legislative amendment in 1939 to specify that the death sentence was not mandatory where an Aboriginal person was convicted of murder, the increasing use of the power of commutation, and the restriction of capital punishment to the crime of murder in 1968. On 5 March 1970, Dick Ward MLC, who was later appointed as a Judge of the Supreme Court of the Northern Territory, introduced a Bill in the Northern Territory Legislative Council providing for the abolition of the death penalty. Debate on the Bill was repeatedly adjourned until it eventually passed on 20 February 1973. During his second reading speech for the Bill, Mr Ward quoted the following passage from George Bernard Shaw's play *Caesar and Cleopatra*:

> "To the end of history, murder shall breed murder, always in the name of right and honour and peace, until the gods are tired of blood and create a race that can understand."

This is the ultimate lesson of Dr Pugh's work, and I congratulate him for his scholarship and insight.

Supreme Court Chambers
December 2025

Preface
A Hanging Carnival

In July 1893 the *Northern Territory Times* was exultant, screaming *"A HANGING CARNIVAL"* in capital letters[1]. What was going on? In the 23 years since white settlement, there had never been a legal hanging. Of course, there had been murders, and trials of the guilty. In fact, death was never very far away. There were numerous retribution massacres, men shot while attempting to escape, deaths from crocodiles, disease, accident and thirst, but few of these ended in a trial. They were all too common, but a hanging *carnival*?

Justice Charles Dashwood had excelled in the court that year. In February he was on the bench for three murder cases in three days. After the juries had declared the accused to be guilty, Dashwood took the bit between his teeth and sentenced ten of them to death.

Fortunately for most of them, Dashwood also had the power to recommend commuting their sentences and eventually did so for all but two of the condemned, and those two did indeed hang for their crime.

Early in the morning of the 14th of July, John Archibald Graham Little, the long-term telegraph and postmaster and deputy sheriff of the tiny South Australian colony of Palmerston, on the north coast of Australia, shared a memo with the press. The date for the executions of the men currently lounging on death row in Fannie Bay Gaol[2] had been set.

First was Charlie Flannigan (aka McManus), who had been

found guilty of murder at his six-hour trial, five months earlier. He had spent the time since then alone in his cell, sketching his memories of working as a stockman in the cattle stations of the north. He would be hanged the very next day, he was told, and Reverend W. A. Millikan arrived to attend to him in his last hours.

The other nine on the row waited. One was a Larrakia man named Warrima, who had killed a Chinese market gardener named Ah Kim in 1892. The rest were a group of eight Iwaidja men who had brutally murdered six Malay fishermen. They were to be hanged and left hanging in their own lands as a warning to their clan: even "tribal Aborigines" would face the full force of the white man's law. The deputy sheriff was to take them some 250 kilometres eastwards along the shores of Arnhem Land to Malay Bay for the execution.

Wandy Wandy[3], Goolarguo, Capoondur, and Mintaedge and the others thus believed that their fate was *"practically settled"*, as the *Times* put it, and they had ten days left to live. But oh, how the South Australian Press howled.

The *South Adelaide Register* thought that hanging the Aborigines would "be a wicked, cruel, and useless act."[4] It would be better to flog them and send them home, where the "poor creatures… would relate how they had suffered." This, the writer reasoned, "would have a more salutary effect than hanging any quantity of them."

Dashwood may have agreed to a certain extent. He was to comment later that "it is very unsatisfactory to say the least of it, that we should be here to try two creatures who stand there utterly ignorant of what is going on."[5]

Plus, there was real concern that capital punishment was unfairly given to the guilty depending on how dark their skin was. About the same time as Flannigan climbed the gallows steps, Charles Page, who had slain his niece, had his sentence commuted to "penal servitude for life."[6] Page was a white man with friends in high places, including Premier John Downer. Flannigan was a brown man with no friends at all. The argument, according to the *Adelaide Observer*, was that if *both* were undoubtedly guilty, they should both be treated the same.

As the paper put it:

… Page was a civilized and fairly educated white man; Flannigan, offspring of a degraded lubra and a probably unrefined European, [who] never had a chance to do well. He was bred in degradation and cradled and trained in lawlessness. Society must be protected against such men; but the scales of justice must weigh equally, and the sins of the less cultured must not be deemed worse than those of the more cultured. Whilst capital punishment is the legal penalty of murder, both Page and Flannigan ought to be handed over to the public executioner, but if the one is spared so should the other be.[7]

And what of the Aborigines who were facing the noose? Wandy Wandy, the English-speaking recidivist, was the only one who seemed to admit the crime and understand the punishment that they were facing. Anyway, much of the evidence was circumstantial, and if the others were *less* guilty than Wandy Wandy, and even if "they are only blackfellows," the *Observer* pointed out that:

… if they are hanged whilst Page escapes the gallows, their fate will make a still darker stain upon our judicial annals than the execution of Flannigan.[8]

The arguments in Adelaide became more bitter. When the decisions of the Executive Council regarding capital punishment were discussed in Parliament, Territory Representative Walter Griffiths and some of his parliamentary colleagues declared that a grave injustice had already been made by hanging Flannigan, and they pressed the Executive Council to rethink their decisions before it was too late.

The *South Australian Chronicle* pointed out that modern attempts for a community to go without capital punishment had only ended in greater crime. In Switzerland, for example, eight of the Swiss cantons had *reintroduced* the death penalty after five years. The long arm of the law, said the *Chronicle*, needed to fall equally across a civilised nation, no matter how far removed, or remote, were the crimes.

Nothing would more swiftly tend to make attempts at civilisation a complete failure than the spread of a conviction that the arm of justice was too short and feeble to reach wrongdoers and inflict upon them the penalty due to their crimes.[9]

But, they reminded their readers, it was a serious affair:

… human life, even though it be that of an aboriginal, is too sacred to be lightly taken away.[10]

Territorians, through their only weekly paper, the *Northern Territory Times and Government Gazette*, appeared bemused by the "antagonistic criticism from the Press of South Australia proper."[11] The paper's editor, Charles Kirkland, felt sure that most Territorians would be in favour of capital punishment. "Not that there is any strong feeling here as to the unqualified merit of the gallows as a deterrent to crime"[12] he suggested, "but it may be argued that while capital punishment remains an institution among us there are certain cases which demand its rigours."[13] Five months before, with ten men on death row, the paper could find no sympathy for Flannigan and encouraged his hanging for, if the sentence was *not* carried out, "the gallows [was] doomed as an instrument of justice in South Australia."[14]

In the end, as we shall see, Wandy Wandy was hanged alone because Dashwood and the Executive Council in Adelaide caved in to the pressure and commuted the sentences of the others. The *Hanging Carnival* thus never occurred, and the arguments for and against capital punishment continued. They were so passionately presented, on both sides, that executions became an increasingly rare event, and it was a brave judge who ordered them.

From 1884 to 1911 the Judge of the Northern Territory exercised the full powers of the Supreme Court under the *Northern Territory Justice Act*. There were four of them: Thomas Pater, Charles Dashwood, Charles Herbert and Samuel Mitchell, and they only dealt with criminal trials. After the administration of the Territory was moved to the Commonwealth of Australia, the Supreme Court of the Northern Territory was established, with Justice David Bevan presiding.

The judicial concern over racism came to a head in 1913. Both Chief Protector of Aboriginals William Stretton and Justice Bevan agreed that there was a problem with the jury system in the Territory because of racism and the small population that was available to draw the jury from.

In a letter to the Administrator[15] in September 1913, Stretton pointed out that two very similar cases had just been tried but had very different outcomes: a white man, Carl Lindroth was acquitted of murdering an Aboriginal man named Dick (after a *three-minute* retirement to discuss the case!), but the Aboriginal men accused of killing a white man named Clare Ernest Campbell were found guilty. Stretton pointed out that five of the jury were the same for both cases and he regretted to say, 'without any hesitation,' that:

> … the verdicts in these cases are inconsistent and in one case at least ill-considered.[16]

Justice Bevan followed up the Protector's letter to the Administrator on 25 September 1913. The three-minute consideration of Lindroth's guilt, or otherwise, he said, was ridiculous:

> To say they "considered" their verdict would be to introduce an element of the farcical into the administration of justice.[17]

Bevan requested a discussion with Administrator John Gilruth about the idea of dispensing with the jury altogether in capital cases because:

> Juries will not convict a white man for an offence against a black, certainly if the evidence is that of blacks, whereas on black evidence, there is no difficulty in the way of securing conviction against a black for an offence against a white man…[18]

I feel confident," he wrote

> … that the judge sitting with two assessors would be far more likely to arrive at an honest decision, than twelve men picked indiscriminately whose sole interpretation of a "White Australia" is that the "nigger" is something a good bit lower than a dog, to be exploited and used for his own particular

purposes.[19]

Gilruth 'candidly' agreed that the jury system was "not suitable for the Territory in its present stage of development"[20] and he held the opinion that the Minister, Judge Bevan and himself should have a personal discussion about the abolition of the jury system. Unfortunately, if this discussion ever took place, it is not in the records, and the jury system continued for another 8 years. It was finally abolished for all crimes except murder in 1921, although this was repealed in 1930.

There were 39 murder trials held in the Palmerston Court between 1884 and 1913, and Justice Bevan provided a list of them to External Affairs Minister Glynn[21] (see Appendix 1) on his request. Some of the accused were acquitted, and of those found guilty and condemned to death, most had their sentences commuted to life in prison.

Such 'luck' continued through the twentieth century: Nemarluk, Minemarra, Mangulmangul, Nargoon, Marragin and Mankee, for example, were all condemned to death in 1933 after being found guilty of the murder of three Japanese fishermen, but each of the sentences was commuted to imprisonment for life. Nemarluk, now famous as an Indigenous resistance leader, died in Fannie Bay Gaol in 1940, possibly of tuberculosis.

Of those who were executed, Flannigan and Wandy Wandy were only the first. Eight others paid the final price for their crimes, and it took eighty years to finally end the practice of capital punishment in the Territory.

Ninety-one years after Flannigan died, all the states and territories in Australia had outlawed the death penalty. The Northern Territory waited until 1973, but the last was Western Australia, in 1984. There, Brenda Hodge was sentenced to death for killing her abusive policeman husband in Kalgoorlie. Luckily for her, her sentence was commuted, and she was paroled in 1995.[22]

There were 114 people legally executed in the Commonwealth

of Australia after Federation in 1901. The last two to hang in Darwin dropped to their deaths at Fannie Bay Gaol in 1952. The last to hang in Australia was Ronald Ryan in 1967, after he had killed a prison guard while escaping from Pentridge Gaol.

Back in 1893, waiting for death in Fannie Bay Gaol, Charlie Flannigan was given paper and pencils in his cell to fill in time, and he is now known for his art as much as the murder of a cattleman. In 2023, Library and Archives Curator Don Christophersen exhibited Flannigan's drawings from his time locked in solitary confinement before his final day. Flannigan must have rolled in his grave!

Christophersen also researched and compiled a book on Charlie Flannigan's story titled *A Little Bit of Justice*, and for the first time in 130 years, Flannigan's life was revealed in all its tragic details.

Christophersen left it to his readers to decide whether the punishment was justified, or whether Flannigan deserved a commuted sentence like most others received. This book does the same with all ten felons who were legally executed in the Northern Territory – six of them condemned by Justice Charles Dashwood.

Murder was not the occupation of any one race, but it was, and is, more likely to be perpetrated by men. In his 9 years on the bench in Darwin, for example, Justice Kriewaldt presided over 39 murder trials involving men. Just over half involved Aboriginal people, but the others were from a range of other groups. His first, in 1952, were the two Czech immigrants who appear in this book. They were hanged for murdering a taxi driver (see Ch 8) and Kriewaldt was so shocked by the event that none of his following 37 murder trials ended in the death penalty. In fact, Kriewaldt became a vocal opponent of it.

Of the ten who were hanged in the Northern Territory, six were Aboriginal men, two were Chinese, and (after a gap of 39 years) two were Czech 'New Australians.' Seven were hanged at Fannie Bay Gaol, and three on the same ground that had witnessed the murders (see Map 1).

The stories of these ten men are rarely told nowadays, but they survive in the archives and newspapers of the times. Discovering them was an adventure.

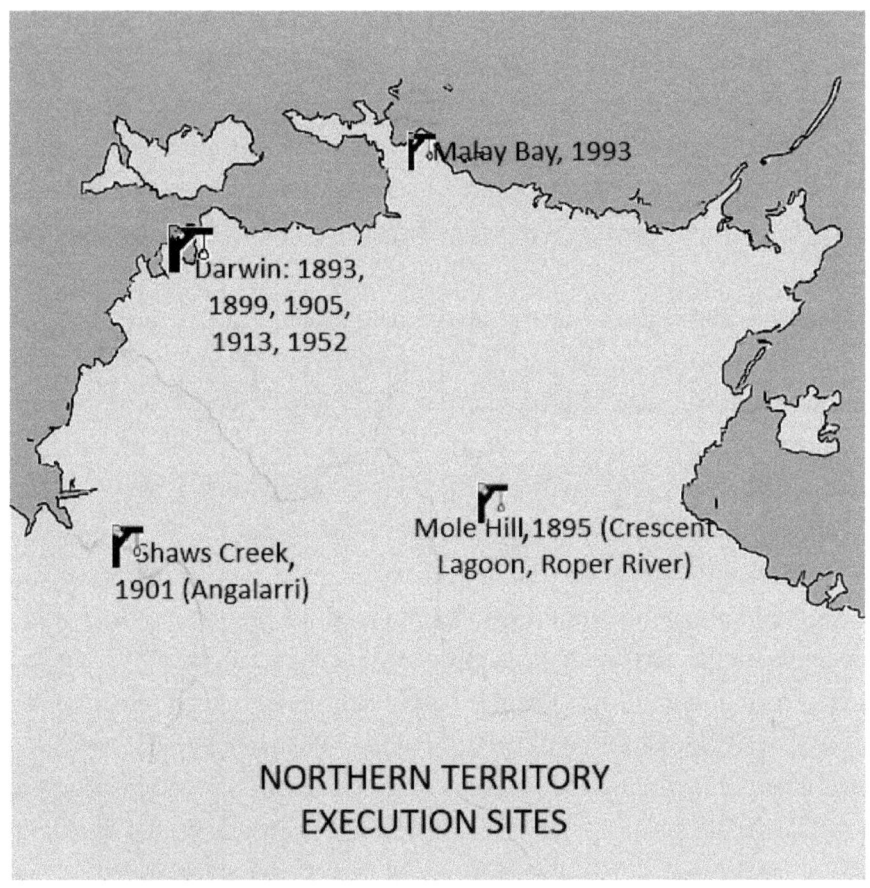

Map 1: Northern Territory Execution sites. Palmerston (Darwin) had seven executions in Fannie Bay Gaol, and three on country – close to the site of the original crimes, as a lesson to the condemned men's clan.

Endnotes

1. *NTTGG*, 14 July 1893, page 2: A Hanging Carnival.
2. Fannie Bay Gaol, is more formally known as 'Her Majesty's Gaol and Labour Prison.'
3. Aka Wandi Wandi.
4. *South Australian Register*, 18 July 1893, page 6: Matthew Goode: Capital Punishment.
5. Peter Elder, *Northern Territory Dictionary of Biography*. Comment made by Dashwood in 1894.
6. *The Express and Telegraph*, 5 July 1893: The Condemned Man.
7. *Adelaide Observer*, 15 July 1893, page 24: White and Black Murderers.
8. *Adelaide Observer*, 15 July 1893, page 24: White and Black Murderers.
9. *South Australian Chronicle*, 8 July 1893, page 4: The Death Penalty.
10. *South Australian Chronicle*, 8 July 1893, page 4: The Death Penalty.
11. *NTTGG*, 14 July 1893, page 2: A Hanging Carnival.
12. In an exhaustive evaluation of the executions in Australia between 1910 and 1973, Vincent O'Sullivan concluded that there was no deterrent effect on crimes following executions (O'Sullivan, 2018).
13. *NTTGG*, July 1893, page 2: A Hanging Carnival.
14. *NTTGG*, 3 March 1893, page 2: Editorial.
15. Stretton to Gilruth, 20 September 1913, NAA: A3, NT1914/426 p 33.
16. Stretton to Gilruth, 20 September 1913, NAA: A3, NT1914/426 p 32.
17. Bevan to Gilruth, 25 September 1913, NAA: A3 NT1914/426 p 25.
18. Bevan to Gilruth, 25 September 1913, NAA: A3 NT1914/426 p 25.
19. Bevan to Gilruth, 25 September 1913, NAA: A3 NT1914/426 p 26.
20. Gilruth to Minister for External Affairs, 27 September 1913, NAA: A3, NT1914/426 p 21.
21. Gilruth to Secretary, Department of External Affairs, 7 January 1914, NAA: A3, NT1914/426 pp 3-5.
22. Hodge, 2005.

Chapter 1
Charlie Flannigan, 1893

Hanged in Fannie Bay Gaol on 15 July 1893, for the murder of Samuel Croker at Auvergne Station in September 1892.

Figure 1: Charlie Flannigan, self-portrait 1892.

Charlie Flannigan was the son of an Irish man and an Aboriginal woman who grew up on stations in the Diamantina region of Queensland. Also called Charlie McManus, he was illiterate but by the time he arrived in the Territory, he was an expert with horses and cattle and was an experienced general station hand. We know he was an excellent horse rider because, when we first hear of him, he was the 'coloured lad' who rode an apparently lame horse named Cygnet to win the 1887 Palmerston Cup:

… there was the additional surprise of Cygnet pulling off the big money "on three legs," after making a holy show of himself in the Hurdle Race by first running off the course and then refusing to take his jumps. Early in the morning this horse was reported to be a "stiff 'un," to use a sporting phrase, and certainly the horse's limping and the gloomy looks of his supporters seemed to justify the rumour that he was thrown out of all engagements. How far he was thrown out may be calculated from the easy manner in which the coloured lad kept him in front from start to finish of the Cup.[1]

Cygnet was owned by Bernard Murphy, the proprietor of the Sportsmans Arms and General Store in Katherine. His prize was 100 sovereigns for the mile and a half race, which was 'called' in the *Northern Standard*:

> Another very good start set the field going for the big money, the Katherine River horse getting a slight advantage. Passing the post the first time round Cygnet was leading, with Hilltop second, Joker third, Duke of Manchester fourth and the colt last, about a length separating each horse. When a mile had been got over, the positions were the same Cygnet drawing away and Joker and the colt drawing up to Hilltop; but at this point No Name bolted from the track. Coming into the straight for home Joker was seen to have collared Hilltop, and was making gamely for the leader, but the chestnut had too much foot, independent of whip or spur, and he finished a length and a half ahead, Hilltop: length away third, Duke of Manchester a good fourth.[2]

Flannigan might have been paid well, and no doubt celebrated his win. He may have then returned to Katherine with Murphy, before continuing to cattle stations on the two horses he owned, looking for work. He also owned a Snider rifle and was an independent traveller through the bush. At one time he worked for the famous drover, Nat 'Bluey' Buchanan, whose son Gordon wrote that Flannigan would do anything for Nat, although "he often resented orders from others."[3]

Flannigan may also have met another famous cattleman about this time, Nat Buchanan's mate, 'Greenhide Sam' Croker, but there would have been no inkling then of the trouble ahead – trouble that would see Croker in his grave, and Flannigan on the gallows.

The Victim

Samuel Burns Croker was a pioneer cattleman. He had grown up on a station near Tamworth, New South Wales, and as a young man worked

Chapter 1: Charlie Flannigan, 1893

on the Hodgkinson Norwest Exploring Expedition in Queensland (1876-7). This was where he first became mates with Nat Buchanan and threw his lot in with him as a cattle drover, stockman and station manager. In fact, he worked for Buchanan on several important long cattle drives, bringing in the early herds of cattle to the Victoria River Region and, when Buchanan founded Wave Hill Station in 1883, it was Croker he left in charge. Three years later, Croker again joined Buchanan, joining their herds near Newcastle Waters, to pioneer the Murranji Track, an important overland route that became a short cut to the west.

Croker was called 'Greenhide Sam' for his skill with working with untanned hides, and he was much admired by the white fraternity in the early stations. Gordon Buchanan knew him well and described him as:

> … fair, of medium height and wiry build ... a natural backwoodsman, hardy and accustomed to hunt for a life on "bush tucker" of all kinds, from dingo and snakes to barramundi and wild duck, his eyes and ears rarely missed the signs of game... Though not a good tracker, he had all the other bush craft of the aborigine... Never enthusiastic, yet never downhearted, he was generally cheerfully imperturbable, with a tendency to romance, and to chaff and banter, which habit led to his sudden and dramatic end.[4]

The admiration of white men did not necessarily follow through to the Aboriginal population of the Northern Territory. Croker was a killer. An "enthusiastic participant"[5] of massacres, he was a member of several reprisal posses, the first of which slaughtered 20 or more Aboriginal people in revenge for the murder of Bill Travers near the Limmen River in 1878.[6]

On another occasion he was readily recruited by the police to join them after the murder of Duncan Campbell, near the Roper River in 1882.[7] This group massacred about 30 men and boys on the banks of Red Lily Lagoon.[8]

Soon after arriving at Wave Hill, Croker is also said to have shot a Gurindji man in the back while he was swimming across a river because he had stolen a bucket.[9] As an aside, here we find an intriguing possibility. This Gurindji man was described as a 'half-caste' about 30 years old. If his father was a white man, he was born decades before white settlement in the region. It begs the question of his origins – the only white men in the area at the time were members of Augustus Gregory's exploration expedition in 1855.[10]

Clearly, Croker was no angel. However, if you asked two well-known station managers in the area at the time who knew him well, they would have told you otherwise. Jack '*The Gulf Hero*' Watson and Lindsay Crawford both held their colleague in high esteem:

"No one could possibly be kinder" said Watson, regarding Croker's "disposition towards the blacks."[11] Watson may never have met Flannigan, but he was prepared to comment on his character for the media:

> According to… these gentlemen, Flannigan is a very low type of half-caste, very little better than an ordinary bush blackfellow.[12]

Lindsay Crawford agreed and similarly praised Croker for his kindness.[13] With the benefit of hindsight, however, we can consider these two cattlemen very poor character witnesses indeed. They stand together at the forefront of the worst killers of Aboriginal people in the Northern Territory's history. Between them, more than a hundred Aboriginal people ended their lives at the wrong end of Winchester or Snider rifles.[14] Jack Watson was particularly well used to massacres. After all, it was *his* shed wall in Queensland where Emily Creagh counted 40 pairs of ears nailed up as trophies in 1882.[15] And Lindsay Crawford is known to have reaped revenge in a similar manner against a clan whose members murdered a cattlemen named Sid Scott in 1892. He made a 'swift and terrible example in a terrible manner':

> … he and his half-caste dealt out white man's justice with their Winchesters, and when the police arrived from Pine Creek a couple of days later, they found plenty of employment burying the sons of darkness.[16]

Chapter 1: Charlie Flannigan, 1893

Massacres were forgiven by most of the white community in those days, and they were never brought before a court of law. Most white men saw the killings as a legitimate response to the murder of one of their fellows, and a lesson to the black man.[17] But when Watson died in the Katherine River in 1896 and his body was never found, it is tempting to think that, perhaps, someone was at last able to take some revenge.[18]

Charlie Flannigan worked for Sam Croker at Wave Hill Station for several months in 1892, mustering cattle. That is how he ended up at Auvergne Station – Croker had taken over its management and had promised Flannigan a job. Before 'the trouble,' he had already spent nine days building a fence for him at Auvergne, with Jock *'Tam O'Shanter'* McPhee.[19]

Gordon Buchanan's 1933 comment about Croker's "chaff and banter," might give a clue to the tipping point that led to Flannigan becoming his killer. Perhaps Croker's banter of the evening compounded deep anger Flannigan held from some previous experience together. Nobody knows, as the motive for the murder was never made clear.

Auvergne Station

Auvergne Station lies about 50 kilometres west of the current town of Timber Creek. Croker had only been there as manager a few weeks as he had taken over from Jack Watson.[20] Flannigan had followed him there after the promise of a job.

On a warm September evening, perhaps with the first signs of the looming 'build-up' on the horizon that heralded the coming wet season, Croker, Flannigan, McPhee and Joe Ah Wah, the cook, were playing cribbage with "the stake of a stick of tobacco a game"[21] on the station veranda. As the grog took its effect, Croker's "chaff and banter" flowed even more freely. We don't know exactly what was said, but Flannigan finally had enough.

During their third game, Flannigan calmly rose, took a drink

Figure 2: Sam Croker's grave is high on the banks of the East Baines River at Auvergne Station.

of water from a cask on the veranda, went out to the saddle shed, returned with his rifle, and shot Croker, twice.

At the trial, an Aboriginal worker named Barney, who was nearby at the time, said he heard Croker sing out 'I am dead' before the second shot. The *Times* was happy to elaborate and assumed he had actually said: "You _____ dog, you have shot me at last."

Joe Ah Wah and McPhee fled, fearing for their lives, but they were back the next morning to bury the body, under Flannigan's direction. Croker was sewn into a blanket by Flannigan himself, with the murderer displaying a "good deal of brutal levity," abusing the corpse with "much coarse profanity in referring to the dead man."[22]

Joe Ah Wah and Barney left Auvergne together and travelled overland to Katherine where they reported the murder to the police. The telegraph master, Robert Murray, then sent a message though to Palmerston:

> Barney, the blackboy who came in with the Chinese cook from Auvergne Station, reports that Croker, McPhee, and the Chinese cook were playing cards in a room at the station, when Yellow Charlie came to the door and fired at Croker with a rifle. The shot took effect in the left side, near the heart. McPhee ran away, as the boy threatened to shoot him

also. The cook seems to have remained. Barney also ran away into the creek. Afterwards they came back to the station and found that Charlie had left in the direction of Hutt River. Croker was found to have two shot wounds, the last one having evidently been fired after he had fallen. Barney says Croker never spoke when the shot was fired. I know nothing further."[23]

Halls Creek

Meanwhile, Flannigan rode westwards to Negri and Ord River Stations. At Ord River, Flannigan met Mortimer Kelly, a station worker he had previously known, and Kelly then accompanied him to Halls Creek, making sure he arrived. He was later interviewed by the police:

> "I was working at the Ord River Station on 27th September, when prisoner rode up. I said, "What's up, Charlie?" He said, "Oh, an accident." He then said, "Where's Booty?" Prisoner went over to Mr. Booty and then came back to the trough where I was to water his horse. I said, "There's something the matter, I can tell; what's up?" He said, "Old Croker threatened to shoot me, so I knocked him over." I said, "What for?" and he replied, "Well, there was an old sore between me and him."[24]

At Halls Creek, Flannigan calmly surrendered himself to the police and gave an oral statement to Sergeant Brophie, who wrote it down in language the courts would understand:

> I met Samuel Croker at Wave Hill Station, Northern Territory, on or about the 23rd July 1892. I had known Croker well before. He offered me employment on the Auvergne cattle station… Croker had gone on before me. I was employed in putting up a fence. I worked two or three days without having any quarrel. I had a few angry words after this in connection with the fence. A man named John McPhee was present at the time. McPhee was working at the fence with me.
>
> The next day following this argument Croker went out with a blackboy to fetch in a bullock to kill it. I and McPhee were working at the yard the next day while the bullock was being

Figure 3: Charlie Flannigan sketched the scene of his arrest, from memory, while waiting on death row (1893, South Australian Museum aa263-1-9a).

killed. Croker rounded up the cattle about 100 yards from where we were working. I heard a shot and saw something strike the ground about ten yards in front of me. I heard two more shots. Croker told me that he missed the bullock first shot but hit him with the other two. I drew McPhee's attention to the first shot and said, "That man is trying to shoot either you or me."

Croker came over after the third shot. I asked him if he was trying to shoot us or the bullock. He said, "No" Croker then gave me the rifle and told me to shoot the bullock. I shot the bullock, and all the others butchered the beast.

I had no further words with Croker that day. We had supper together. I spoke to him once or twice, but he did not answer me. I had breakfast with Croker in the morning. I had words with him then. McPhee and I then went out to work at the yard. We had been working for about a quarter of an hour when Croker came down. He started growling at me about a log which I had been morticing – he said I was not doing it right. I made no reply. He told me then to go and get an axe and sharpen it and cut some stakes, and I did so.

I came back at dinner time, but they had finished dinner, and I had mine with the Chinaman cook. I went away after dinner

Chapter 1: Charlie Flannigan, 1893

and cut some more stakes, coming back at supper time. I had supper with the Chinaman. There was some beef smoking in a shed, and Croker said to me, "You had better go down and get a bit of cow dung," and I did so.

I came back and sat on Croker's bunk. Croker said, "What the hell are you doing sitting on my bunk?"

I never said anything but got off his bunk. Croker said, "Don't sit on my bunk anymore!" and I replied, "All right."

I walked outside and sat down on an old bunk. Shortly afterwards I went over to the kitchen. The Chinaman cook asked me to have a game of crib, and I played with him for a good while. Then McPhee and Croker came in, and McPhee suggested a four-hand game and cut for partners. Croker and I, according to the cut, should have been partners, but he would not play with me, consequently I took the Chinaman as a partner. I held 15—8 in my hand, also two 10's. Croker said, "You bloody fool you have got fourteen in your hand." We were playing for a stick of tobacco a game.

Croker said, "You thick-headed b——r, count them over again."

I said, "They are there; ten and no more."

Then Croker said, "You bloody bastard, what do you know about cards?" adding, "You b——r, I'll brain you."

I said, "If I am a bastard I'll have a fight at you."

He then said, "I can't fight, but I will bloody well shoot you."

I threw up my cards and ran and got my rifle, which was in a bough shed about 15 yards distant from where we were sitting. I got the rifle and leaded it – it was a Snider – and came back with it and asked him whether he was going to do it. He jumped up to rush to his camp. He had no firearms on him and nothing in his hands. As he was running to his camp I shot at him. He was sideways on, and I shot him in the chest, and he fell down. He never spoke afterwards. McPhee and the Chinaman cook, one blackboy, two gins and a child ran into the bush. I remained with Croker.

McPhee came back in about an hour and was leading a gin by the hand. This happened at about 7 or 8 o'clock in the evening of about the 20th September 1892.

McPhee said when he came up, "I suppose it is all right now?"

and I said "Yes; I suppose it's all right if you don't knock me down."

We went back to where Croker was lying and rolled him up in his blanket. The Chinaman cook did not come back till next morning. After breakfast we all went down and dug a grave and buried him. The next morning, I went out and got my horse with the intention of clearing out into the bush. McPhee also sent for his horses in order to go and inform the police. I asked him if I should go in with him, and he said, "The best thing you can do is to go into the bush."

I did so, taking my rifle and a few cartridges. After being a few days in the bush, I felt very lonely, and had been thinking about what I had done. I then said to myself, I'll go into the nearest station and see what is the best thing to do, I did so, going into the Negri Station. When I got there, I found I knew the man in charge, and I told him what I had done. His name is Joseph Stephens. He took the rifle from me and advised me to go and give myself up to the police. He gave me a letter to Mr. Booty, the manager of the head station. I went to Mr. Booty, and he also advised me to give myself up. He sent a man on with me to Hall's Creek."[25]

Sergeant Brophie then escorted Flannigan overland from Halls Creek to Wyndham, and he was extricated to Darwin by steamer. In those days the road to Wyndham was little more than a 400-kilometre cart track through the bush used by gold miners and cattlemen. On horseback it took more than a week to traverse, and Flannigan would have been kept in chains, particularly at night, to ensure he did not escape. Travelling the track was not for the faint-hearted. Strong miners pushed wheelbarrows if they could not afford horses, and there were plenty of them – Halls Creek had a population of about 500 people by 1886. Not everyone survived, and those who fell by the wayside were usually discovered by other travellers. For example, a man named Ludwick was found in 1886:

> … about forty miles from [Halls Creek]. It appears that the man had left town well equipped with horses and rations, but it is surmised that the heat, which has been very great lately, overpowered him, and he lay down and died.[26]

Chapter 1: Charlie Flannigan, 1893

But Brophie managed Flannigan's transport without incident, and Flannigan was duly chained to the superstructure of the SS *Adelaide* for the crossing of the Joseph Bonapart Gulf to Darwin. Brophie delivered his prisoner and returned to Wyndham, leaving Flannigan in the custody of Inspector Paul Foelsche.

The Police Court

Flannigan appeared, undefended, before Foelsche's Police Court in the first week of December. Foelsche's job was to decide if there was evidence enough to send the prisoner to trial. Flannigan had confessed, but he nevertheless pleaded not guilty.

Joe Ah Wah and Barney gave their recollections of the events. Their testimonies were published in detail by the local newspaper.[27]

Ah Wah said he did not actually see the killing:

… I next heard the report of a rifle shot, and I saw the blaze come from the barrel; the blaze came around the corner, from the direction of the shed; it was very close; the blaze was nearest to kitchen; when I saw the blaze I jumped up and ran away into the kitchen, and got into the corner amongst some bags of flour; I saw Croker's head near the kitchen door, and heard some bubbling; heard someone coming in at the front door of the kitchen; heard the rattle of a rifle being loaded or unloaded; I then heard another shot; this second shot was fired inside the kitchen; it was fired straight at Sam Croker; it was fired from a very close distance, but I could not see who fired it; I then jumped through the kitchen window and ran into the bush.[28]

Barney's story was similar, but he had been outside in the shed:

… I remember being at the shed with two lubras; I heard them playing cards outside the kitchen; they were using a fat lamp; by and by I saw Charley come to the shed, but he did not speak to me; he took Sam Croker's rifle and got two cartridges; after that I heard two shots; I saw the prisoner take the cartridges and go to a tree close by the kitchen; after the shot was fired I heard Sam Croker sing out "I am dead"; I heard and saw prisoner fire two shots; I then ran away to the creek because I was frightened he would shoot me.²⁹

These testimonies were enough for Inspector Foelsche to remand Flannigan for a 'pre-trial' on a date set three weeks later, but this was delayed "by means of many adjournments … until the 2nd of February," when McPhee's evidence was taken.

> … We were waiting for prisoner to come and finish the game. I next heard the report of a rifle in the direction where prisoner had gone, quite close to me, and saw Croker put both hands to his side and stagger towards me, saying, "You bloody dog, you have shot me at last." Croker then staggered towards the kitchen door, and fell, and struggled on the floor. Joe went into the kitchen, and I also rushed through the house. I said to Joe, " Don't make a d—d fool of yourself." I went towards the shed and saw prisoner loading his rifle. I was within two feet of him.³⁰

McPhee's statement detailed the aftermath of the incident. It gives the suggestion of a motive, but it was not something that was followed up by the court:

> … I rushed through the shed. I saw some blacks running away, and I followed them towards the river. When I got there, I heard another shot fired.
>
> I had no firearms. I went to the stockyard, and after a few minutes saw Barney. I and the two lubras then went back to the house. I saw prisoner lying in front of the shed with a rifle in his right hand. I spoke to him and asked him if he was finished, or if he wanted any more to say.
>
> Prisoner said, "No; I would sooner cut my b——y throat than shoot either you or Joe, for you have never done me any harm."
>
> I asked him where Joe was, and he said, "He's all right, I heard him going through the bush." Prisoner was walking about at this time. He said, " That old b——r has done me a lot of harm."
>
> He then asked me to get a rug to cover Sam up with. I said, "Wait till Annie comes." She was one of the lubras. Prisoner and I then went to where Croker was lying.
>
> Prisoner had his rifle. Told him I didn't like it, and he said,

"You needn't be afraid." I then heard Annie sing out, and she and Barney came. I then got a rug and spread it out on the verandah near Croker's body. I saw a wound in the head and in the left side of the body. They were bullet wounds.

There was a lot of blood where the body was lying. I did not touch the body. He was quite dead. Prisoner and Barney then lifted the body onto the rug and covered it over. This was about 11 o'clock. We then went to bed.

Joe Waugh was away. We got up at daybreak next morning. Prisoner also got up and stretched himself, and said, "Thank God! another day and I am still alive."

I lit a fire and boiled the billy. Prisoner was talking, but I forget what he said. I got another can and went up to the yard to milk the cow. Prisoner sang out, "Jack, where are you going?" I said, "Going to milk the cow."

He said, "Don't be long, and Barney, you stay with me."

The three lubras went with me. I saw Joe there, and when I had milked the cow, we returned to the house. Prisoner was still there with Barney. Prisoner and Joe were talking. The three of us then had breakfast.

Afterward I said, "We had better dig the grave before it gets too hot." We all went to do it. After digging it we all went back to where Croker's body was lying. Prisoner then sewed the rug around the body, addressing the body, "If I hadn't done this you would have had the pleasure of sewing me up."

Part of Croker's face was exposed. We got some galvanized iron and bent them up for a coffin, and prisoner and I placed the body in it and tied it up with rope. We then carried the body to the grave and lowered it down.

Prisoner then said, "You old b———r, you are better there than a young fellow like me." We then started to fill up the grave. Prisoner said, " That's enough for the old b———r," I said, "No, I will finish it."

Prisoner said, "All right, you will be paid for it, but I won't – I am a murderer."

After finishing we all went back to the house and had dinner. I then went and lay down in the shed. Prisoner came and spoke to me and said, "Jack, you seem downhearted over this affair."

Figure 4: Darwin Court House on the Esplanade, 1893 (ph0238-0734, LANT, Peter Spillet Collection).

I said, "No, I am not."

He said, "You needn't be; it's an old affair." The same evening prisoner said, "Croker has carried a revolver for a fortnight for the purpose of killing me."

We had supper and all went to bed.[31]

The Circuit Court

Foelsche committed Flannigan to trial at the Circuit Court, presided over by Justice Charles Dashwood, two weeks later.[32]

THURSDAY, FEB. 16 MURDER

Charlie Flannigan, alias McManus a half-caste native of Australia, was charged with the willful murder of one Samuel Croker at Auvergne Station in the month of October last.

Mr. Symes defended, and prisoner pleaded not guilty.

Jury: V. V. Brown, H. M. Debross, H. H. Adcock, G. McKeddie, M. D. Armstrong, P. R. Freer, A. A. Lewis, S. R. Budgen, H. Dudeney, R. R. Rundle, D. Daniels, and A. E. Jolly.

This trial occupied from 10 a.m. to 4 p.m. and being so near to time of publication we cannot oblige distant readers with the evidence this week. It is only necessary to say here that the evidence for the Crown was complete and not shaken in any point by cross-examination.

Mr. Symes called no evidence for the defence and did not think it necessary to put prisoner in the box.

Prisoner made no statement whatever either before or after the verdict, and except for a smile or two while the Judge was summing up manifested little or no interest in the proceedings, although perfectly understanding all that was going on. His Honor summed up very fully, occupying quite an hour in doing so. The jury were not long in arriving at a unanimous verdict of guilty of willful murder.[33]

Flannigan was returned to Fannie Bay Gaol in chains. Death row meant that he had a cell to himself, with very little time out of it.

Flannigan presented no evidence at his six-hour trial and appeared indifferent throughout regarding his fate. Perhaps this indifference made it easier for Justice Dashwood to order his execution, despite the undiscovered motive:

> Before passing sentence, His Honor addressed the prisoner in very severe terms, characterizing him as one of the most cruel and cowardly criminals that had ever come before him. He held out no hope of mercy to the prisoner, who was finally sentenced to death in the usual way. At the passing of the sentence prisoner showed no sign of emotion.[34]

During the next five idle months, Flannigan requested paper and pencils to sketch scenes from memory. When Reverend Millikan questioned him, Flannigan expressed regret for his past, and said he was 'sorry for the life he had led but hoped it would be all right where he was going'. He was uncertain if he'd end up "a stoker in Hell or come back with wings."

The Gallows

According to *The Advertiser*, Flannigan:

> … freely acknowledged his guilt and manifested no fear. He walked to the scaffold with a firm step, saying he was going 'to die hard.' The execution, which was the first that has taken place in the Northern Territory, was carried out without a hitch, death being instantaneous.[35]

The authorities were relieved. It was important that everything went well – they had put a lot of effort into not messing up their first hanging to avoid any 'unseemly hitches and a revolt of public sentiment'. The second-hand gallows had been sent from Adelaide Gaol especially.[36] They were erected in the open:

> … in the yard between the cells and the infirmary. So that there might be no mishap, the beam and rope were tested several times, with as much as double the weight of the doomed man. That fatal act, the drawing of the bolt, was practiced, too, until perfection was assured. Beneath the trapdoor a deep excavation had been made to prevent the man's feet touching ground after the drop; and across the front of the structure, below the platform, a screen of calico had been tacked.[37]

With the rest of the prisoners watching, Flannigan was brought from his cell at 9 a.m. with his arms 'pinioned'. He was able to walk freely, but he was closely attended by the gaoler, Norcock, and several guards:

> … He was halted for a few minutes in the dining room close by, while the needful formalities of identification of prisoner and his delivery to the Deputy-Sheriff were gone through. Physically, he looked strong and healthy. He had spent a good night and actually slept up till half past 7 o'clock. He partook of the usual breakfast, and just before going forth to his doom enjoyed a smoke. Whilst the transfer from Gaoler to Sheriff was being made the half-caste betokened not the slightest concern. He never once betrayed a sign that he was going to his death but stood up in his place as stoical as an Indian, and when the Deputy Sheriff had taken him over and the signal was given to adjourn to the scaffold, he walked out with the firm step of a man going to freedom rather than of one about to be killed. [38]

At this point, Flannigan was said to be a "cool customer" who told the hangman how "to make and adjust the knot."

> … Up the steps to the platform, he ascended with the same unalterable coolness, and placing himself on the trapdoor, he stood erect and for a second or two surveyed the yard and those in front of him while the hangman bound his legs with

Chapter 1: Charlie Flannigan, 1893

Figure 5: Wave Hill Homestead by Charlie Flannigan, drawn while waiting on death row (1893, South Australian Museum aa263-1-9a).

rope. That being done, the noose was adjusted, and the black cap drawn over his face…

Then the signal was given, the bolt was drawn, there was a clanging of bolts for an instant, and the spirit of the murderer flashed into eternity. A drop of 6ft had been allowed and death was instantaneous, the only thing noticeable after the body dropped being a slight muscular trembling in the feet. The neck was not torn by the rope, and there was but the merest discolouration visible. After the usual lapse of time, during which we were given every opportunity of viewing the body, it was cut down, and death was duly certified to by the Medical Officer.

… The body was buried in the gaol cemetery, and the lowering of the black flag wiped out the last outward visible trace of the murder of Samuel Croker and the prison and judicial associations of Charley Flannigan, the first man to undergo execution by hanging in the Northern Territory.[39]

Endnotes

1. *North Australian*, 6 August 1887, page 3: N.T. Racing Club. – Fifth Annual Meeting.
2. *North Australian*, 6 August 1887, page 3: N.T. Racing Club. – Fifth Annual Meeting
3. G. Buchanan, 1933.
4. Gordon Buchanan, 1933.
5. Smith 2024.
6. Reid, 1990.
7. *NTTGG*, 7 October 1882, page 3: Murder of Duncan Campbell at Mutka Water Holes.
8. Smith, 2004.
9. Smith, 2004.
10. Lewis, 2004.
11. *NTTGG*, 28 October 1892: Murder in the Northern Territory.
12. *NTTGG*, 7 October 1892, page 3: Murder of Samuel Croker by Half-Caste.
13. *NTTGG*, October 1892: Murder in the Northern Territory. See also Pugh 2023.
14. See Lewis, 2004, 2024; Pugh 2021, 2023; Roberts 2009: Creagh 1883.
15. Creagh 1883.
16. *North Queensland Herald*, 20 May 1911: The Sketcher. Graves on the Outer Edge.
17. Roberts 2005.
18. Jack Watson disappeared while swimming the Katherine River on 1 April 1896. He was transporting supplies across the river to the town, and it is unclear whether he was drowned, or taken by a crocodile, because his body was never recovered. Watson was described as "a fearless and clever horseman…a rough diamond…who was guided by a spirit of daring almost amounting to recklessness… the natives more than once received terribly severe lessons" from Watson and "his ideas of revenge for murders or station depredations committed by the blacks were scarcely orthodox but they were generally up to requirements." *NTTGG*, 10 April 1896, page 3: The Drowning of Mr. J. Watson.
19. Tam O'Shanter was a character in Jeanie Gunn's *We of the Never Never*. He was based on Jock McPhee when he was a stockman at Elsie Station (*Northern Standard*, 18 February 1936, page 7: Characters of "*We of The Never Never*"). McPhee, who was to die of thirst a few yards from water on the Katherine to Willeroo trail in 1910, took up Willeroo Station in 1906. He also appears in NT history as the complainant against Ayaiga ('Tracker Neighbour'), saying that he had robbed his camp. Mounted Constable Johns arrested him but was to be saved by his prisoner after he was knocked off his horse in a flooded river. In a daring rescue, Ayaiga entered the water despite being weighed down by neck chains. He later received the Albert Medal for Bravery from King George V.
20. *NTTGG*, 7 October 1892, page 3: Murder of Samuel Croker by a Half-caste.
21. *NTTGG*, 9 December 1892, page 3: Law Courts, Police Court.
22. *NTTGG*, 21 July 1893, page 3: Murder of Samuel Croker.

23 *NTTGG*, 7 October 1892, page 3: Murder of Samuel Croker by a Half-caste.
24 *NTTGG*, 24 February 1893, page 3: Murder of Samuel Croker.
25 *NTTGG*, 24 February 1893, page 3: Murder of Samuel Croker.
26 *West Australian*, 23 December 1886, page 3, Wyndham Notes.
27 *NTTGG*, 9 December 1892, page 3: Police Court.
28 *NTTGG*, 9 December 1892, page 3: Police Court.
29 *NTTGG*, 9 December 1892, page 3: Police Court.
30 *NTTGG*, 10 February 1893, page 3: Murder of Samuel Croker.
31 *NTTGG*, 10 February 1893, page 3: Murder of Samuel Croker.
32 *NTTGG*, 21 July 1893, page 3: First Northern Territory Execution.
33 *NTTGG*, 17 February 1893, page 3: Law Courts, Circuit Court, Palmerston.
34 *NTTGG*, 17 February 1893, page 3: Law Courts, Circuit Court, Palmerston.
35 *The Advertiser*, 17 July 1893, page 3: The Execution of Flannagan, Death Instantaneous
36 These gallows were replaced with a second set (that were destroyed in the 1937 cyclone). Both these gallows were in the open as all prisoners had to watch the execution. The third gallows, which were only used in 1952, were built inside the infirmary building and are still on display.
37 *NTTGG*, 21 July 1893, page 3: First Northern Territory Execution.
38 *NTTGG*, 21 July 1893, page 3: First Northern Territory Execution.
39 *NTTGG*, 21 July 1893, page 3: First Northern Territory Execution.

Hanged: Execution in the Top End

Chapter 2
Wandy Wandy, 1893

Hanged at Malay Bay on 25 July 1893 for his part in the murder of six Malay fishermen.

Wandy Wandy[1] was an Iwaidja man from the Croker Island/Cobourg Peninsula area who was well known to the Palmerston establishment. He had already spent a decade in Fannie Bay Gaol after he murdered Thomas Howard Wingfield in December 1879. Wingfield was a partner with E. O. (Edward) Robinson in the business of trepang collection and processing for the Chinese market and they were experimenting in commercial tobacco plantations along the coast. They employed about 30 local Iwaidja men and were optimistic about the future of their business. Wandy Wandy was not one of their employees.

Wingfield kept the wages for his employees in his storehouse: flour, rice, tobacco, and rum, and his initial trouble, unsurprisingly, started with the rum.

One morning, an employee named Mayuna arrived to sell some jungle fowl eggs. Wingfield paid him five sticks of tobacco and a little rum, which he rapidly consumed. He then wanted more, and returned to the homestead, drunk, to demand it. Annoyed, Wingfield set his dogs on Mayuna and took out his revolver, possibly just as a threat, but when someone else threw a spear (later claimed to be at a pigeon) near the homestead, Wingfield was startled and he shot Mayuna dead on his veranda.

The clan were furious, and all that day the call for revenge grew among the Iwaidja. Wandy Wandy was chosen to act on the clan's behalf, and he killed Wingfield as he slept that evening – hitting his head three times with a tomahawk. In a letter sent to Alfred Searcy, Edward Robinson recalled the shock of arriving home:

> … Wingfield was killed by the natives while I was in Port Darwin. It was a knock for me on my return to find nothing but the cat to welcome me, the dwelling ransacked, and the poor old chap buried in the sand about six yards from the house. Part of his face was exposed, and the fowls were pecking at it. I had only two black boys with me, and the venture was given up.[2]

Wandy Wandy was arrested and tried for murder. At that time the Territory court was not entitled to try a capital offence, so the death sentence was not an option. Instead, Wandy Wandy was found guilty of manslaughter and sentenced to 10 years hard labour.[3] He escaped soon after, and after he was caught, he was punished by having to spend the next 12 months of his sentence in irons.[4]

During those ten years, Wandy Wandy learned to speak English and joined the Catholic Church. When he was eventually released, he took up residence at the Rapid Creek Mission with Father Donald MacKillop, and lived there quietly for some months before returning home to his countrymen.[5] Unfortunately, back in his own country, Wandy Wandy soon found trouble.

The Victims

When Matthew Flinders explored the Arnhem Land coast in 1803, he met Makassan trepang fishermen in a fleet of praus. He spoke with a captain named Pobasso and discovered that he had been coming to the Arnhem Land coast, which he called "Marege,"[6] for some twenty years. Because Pobasso claimed he was among the first to start the annual trepang collecting migration, some historians date the start of the trepang fishing trips to the 1780s.[7] From then, the Makassan fleet would arrive every year on the seasonal winds, set up camps along the coast, and collect, cook, and dry their prized trepang, a type of sea-slug, for the Chinese market.

The regular contact with the outside world meant there were opportunities for trade and cultural contact between the visitors and the local clans. The clans gained steel tools and cultural items, and knowledge of new skills, while the Makassans obtained the valuable trepang with the help of Aboriginal labour, resources and local knowledge. By the end of the trade in 1906, this enduring, centuries-long cultural exchange left a legacy of shared stories, songlines, and archaeological traces, such as tamarind trees and pottery shards along much of the northern coastline. Unknown numbers of Aborigines travelled on the praus to Makassar (Sulawesi) for the off-season, so many were able to speak Malay.

Because the practice was so long-standing, it is tempting to think that the contact between the two cultures was always respectful and peaceful. But, of course, it wasn't.

In 1892, a single prau, with a crew of six men whose names are long forgotten, was either separated from the fleet or was a separate entity altogether.[8] The fishermen may have landed their prau to make repairs, as it was later said to "be broken," on a beach named Mandool in Malay Bay. There they met a small band of local men, among whom was Wandy Wandy.

Very soon, the Makassans lay dead, and eight men were wanted for murder. Six of them were arrested reasonably quickly. Alfred Searcy, a customs inspector who authored several books on his life in the Top End, was able to accompany the police party on the SS *Adelaide* and he later presented his story of the massacre in his book *In Northern Seas*.[9]

Searcy described how the party landed at Cape Brogden and were led by a local guide named Mangerippy to a "beautiful piece of jungle close to a pretty lagoon,[10] covered with lilies."[11] There they dug up six rotting corpses, and for evidence, took the skulls.

The question of how to carry them, for they were not nice

carrying, arose. I noticed that one of our niggers had on a pair of trousers. These were quickly unshipped and the ends of the legs tied up. We then put three skulls into each leg, and hung them around the nigger's neck, so the question of transport was soon settled.[12]

The police and several trackers then went searching for the killers while Searcy waited on the ship. When he next saw the party at Malay Bay, they had six prisoners: Wandy Wandy, Capoondur, Ingeewaraky, Dooramite, Mintaedge and Angareeda.

The guide, *Mangerippy*, was involved too. He testified at the Police Court:

> I live sometimes at Bowen Straits, sometimes in other parts of that district. I remember going with other blackfellows, including all the prisoners, to Mandool, and seeing Malays there and a proa which had been broken; there were six Malays; at first the Malays spoke, but we did not understand and they then said "Tingha," and pointed towards Bowen Straits; blackfellow say "Take 'em," and then we started to show them the way to Bowen Straits; the prisoner Capoondur suggested that we should kill them, and another of the prisoners said the same; we took the Malays to a swamp and stopped there to eat some cabbage palm; many of the blackfellows carried boxes up from the beach, like those produced in court; the Malays carried guns, but no boxes; they also carried revolver, bow and arrows, and the knives produced; after dinner they walked again towards Robinson's camp; then two of the blackfellows who were carrying boxes, Marakite and Goolardno, ran away, taking the boxes with them; then by-an-by all the blackfellows carrying boxes, including the prisoners, ran away, taking the boxes with them; I stopped a little while, and sang out to the blacks to come back, and then I ran away too; I took the box I was carrying back to the old camp at the swamp; when I got back to the camp all the prisoners were there, also Arramboon; we sat down a little while and then the Malays came back: when the Malays came back they sat down along with the blackfellows: the Malays did not want to fight and did not growl at the blackfellows; the blacks then talked among themselves about killing the Malays; all the prisoners said "Kill them."

Chapter 2: Wandy Wandy, 1893

I said "You no kill 'em"; Arramboon also say, "No kill 'em"; then the blackfellows went into the bush and cut sticks, the Malays remaining sitting down at the camp; Mintaedge was the first to talk about cutting sticks; they cut the sticks and came back to the camp; then Wandy Wandy took away the knife, bow and arrows, and revolver from the Malay captain, and Dooramite took two guns away from a Malay man; then they run away a little distance and stop there: Capoondur then hit the captain on the back of the head with a stick; the captain was sitting down and died at once; Mintaedge hit another Malay with a stick on the back of the head and killed him dead; Angareeda killed another same way; Goolardno killed another with a tomahawk, hitting him across the face: Marakite killed another with a stick; one Malay ran away, and Ingeewaraky threw a stick at him but did not hit him; Goolardno then killed him; after they were all dead Goolardno told me to go and spear the dead men, and I did; then Marakite told Arramboon to go and hit the dead men with a stick, and he did.

After the Malays were killed we made holes and buried the bodies; we put three bodies in one hole, another body in a hole close by, another close to that, and another a little distance away; we then went away to the beach; we went and burnt the proa; all the prisoners were there, also Arramboon; the blackfellows burnt the proa because they were afraid some whitefellow might see it: it was Capoondur that talked that way; we then went back to the swamp where we killed the Malays; we took the Malays' boxes, also arms, and other things, and went to another swamp, where we slept for the night; it was in the afternoon that we burnt the proa.

Next day we went to a fresh water creek called Wark; I saw Prince, Larrakin, and Big Jack at Wark some time afterwards: all the prisoners were there, also lubras and children; I saw Mintaedge give Larrakin a box; the box produced (marked A) is the one: Mintaedge said to Larrakin that he had killed a Malay and got the box; Mintaedge told Larrakin not to tell anybody that he had killed a Malay; Mintaedge then gave Big Jack a knife and sarong; I was close up when he gave it; he told Big Jack he killed the Malay and took the knife and sarong from him: they were like those produced (marked B); I saw

Constable Holdaway at Bowen Straits: I went and showed him where the bodies were buried; Arramboon and others also went: we took up the heads belonging to the bodies; I went and showed where the proa was burnt; the wood produced is some of that belonging to the proa; when the blacks killed the Malays they left the sticks lying about at the camp at the swamp; they were sticks like the one produced.[13]

Rumours ran rife, and people in Darwin were soon talking about a potential massacre in the east. It was confirmed in October 1892, by E. O. Robinson, and it was then that Inspector Foelsche led the police posse to the area in search of the culprits.

The Police Court

They were back in Palmerston by November, accompanied by the accused and several witnesses they had coerced into joining them. Very soon the story was appearing in the press. Six of the accused were charged at the Police Court on 13 November 1892:

… Six aboriginal natives named respectively: Wandy Wandy [sic], Capoondur, Ingeewaraky, Dooramite, Mintaedge, and Angareeda were charged with the wilful murder of six Malays at Mandool, near Bowen Straits…[14]

…. Wandy Wandy… made the following statement, which we render as near as possible in his own pidgin-English: I sit down at Wanmook: all about blackfellow go along Mandool; Capoondur first time go: him go first along beach and find 'em proa; other blackfellows come up behind; Capoondur then said he been find 'em Malay him been break 'em proa; then all blackfellow say 'Come on, we go down and see 'em'; all blackfellows go and see them and I come up behind; the Malays made signs to take the parcels and we all went a little way and got dinner; after we have dinner we take 'em everything away and walk; Malay and me go easy; two fellow, Goolardno and Marakite, go first time and him run away; then me hear Mangerippy sing out "What for you run away;" then all about blackfellow run away; then we go back where make 'em camp before; me sit down; Goolardno yabber me first time "You and me kill 'em all about" and all blackfellow say "All right, kill 'em;" then me sit down little while and Goolardno yabber longa me; he say "You take away that revolver and knife and I kill 'em"; then I sit down little bit and by and by get up and catch 'em that revolver and one knife; then me run away a little way; Dooramite catch 'em two fellow gun and bow and arrow and sit down longa me; then blackfellow kill 'em all about Malays; Goolardno kill 'em two fellow first and Capoondur kill one fellow; then Mintaedge kill another one; Angareeda and Marakite kill one fellow…[15]

The Circuit Court

The trial began on 14 February 1893, with Justice Dashwood presiding and Mr. N. Waters prosecuting. The accused were defended by Reginald Stow, and he immediately applied to separate Wandy Wandy from the others and try him separately because of the man's previous record, but this was disallowed. The jury was sworn in by Justice Dashwood – twelve men whose names appear often in the court reports as jurymen because Palmerston was, after all, a small town.[16] They heard the full story, or as much as was known, and the public read a synopsis of the crime in the papers the next week:

> … a tribe of blacks went to a place known to them as Mandool beach, in Bowen Straits, where they saw a proa which had been wrecked and six Malays who had got ashore from the vessel. A conversation took place between the parties, with the result that the blacks agreed to direct the Malays to Tingha's camp at Port Essington.
>
> Scarcely had they become acquainted with each other when the blacks began to talk of killing the Malays. However, they went some distance towards Tingha's, had a meal en route, and on resuming their journey the blacks who were carrying the boxes, &c, belonging to the Malays, bolted into the bush and returned to their camp. The Malays followed.
>
> The blacks then deliberately went into the bush, cut waddies, and returning to the place where the Malays were resting, cruelly set about their murder, which, so far as shown by the evidence, was entirely unprovoked. Nor was it shown that the Malays resisted in any way the murderous intentions of the

blacks, or, indeed, that they had the opportunity of resistance. They appear to have been surrounded by a host of aboriginals, of whom the prisoners formed only a portion.

After the murder, the prisoners returned to the proa, which they looted and burnt, and then they went again to the scene of the massacre and buried the bodies of the Malays in graves they dug for the purpose.

After this they went off with the property which they had secured and divided it up amongst the members of the local tribes. Some months later rumours of this murder reached Tingha and Mr. E. O. Robinson, who lives near the scene, and in good time the police were apprised of it. Hence the trial.[17]

The court found that Wandy Wandy was the ringleader of the group and although he had killed none of them personally, he had disarmed the Malays before they were attacked.

The trial lasted from 10 a.m. to 6 p.m. There was no evidence presented by the defence, and the summing up by Stow and Justice Dashwood took very little time indeed.

The jury retired at 5 o'clock, but they were back five minutes later with a verdict of wilful murder against the eight prisoners.

Prisoners were then asked in the usual way if they had any statement to make before sentence was passed. Only one of them – Wandy Wandy – ventured any remarks. This prisoner faced His Honor [sic], and in clear and fluent broken English told his story. It was different in some respects to that made at the Police Court by the same man. He protested that when the blacks first came upon the Malays, they were disposed to be unfriendly and cautioned the blacks not to interfere with them under pain of having their hands cut off with knives. He further stated that, at a subsequent period the Malays actually fired two shots at some of the blacks. But in the end, he returned to his original statement, which is so familiar to our readers, in which the manner of the crime was fully and freely set out.

Silence was proclaimed in the usual way, and His Honor then, dispensing with the formality of assuming the black cap, passed the death sentences. He began with Wandy Wandy and served the prisoners one at a time. This terrible duty occupied eight minutes, during which time the profound silence observed, coupled with the solemnity and fearful character of the words spoken, made the situation intensely impressive.

Wandy Wandy exhibited some slight feeling after being condemned to death, but of the remainder it may safely be said that they did not have a very clear conception of the punishment allotted to them. After the eighth had been sentenced the prisoners were removed and the Court closed for the day.[18]

The only hope for the eight men was the chance of the Executive Council deciding to commute their sentences to imprisonment. How much Wandy Wandy's co-offenders understood their potential futures can only be guessed at. Unlike Wandy Wandy, none of them spoke English and the chains that bound them, the locked doors in prison, and the strange culture of the court – with bewigged white men in flowing black robes making judgement on them – must have been very frightening indeed.

For months before the execution, the looming event had been discussed in great depth in every newspaper and, no doubt, in every bar room from Adelaide to Palmerston. In March it looked like the Executive Council would hang four of the eight accused (Wandy Wandy, Goolarguo, Capoondur, and Mintaedge) and pardon the other four. Many people found that odd: "To many minds the half that are pardoned are guilty in like proportion to the ones condemned to die" said the *Times*' editorial,[19] but people were told to consider the educational advantage of hanging four men:

> …the execution at Bowen Straits is intended to be a lesson and a warning to the black natives of that part, and that being so they will derive quite as much learning from the spectacle of four being put to death as they would from seeing eight or even eighty of their fellows hanged… The wisdom of permitting the tribesmen of the criminals to witness the white man's reading of the old Mosaic law cannot be gainsaid.[20]

In the end, seven of the killers had their death sentences

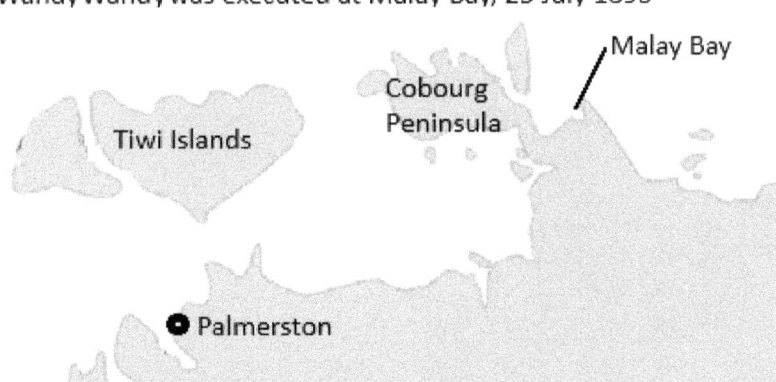

Map 2: Malay Bay is about 350 km northeast of Palmerston.

commuted, and they were sent to prison in Adelaide. Only Wandy Wandy, the recidivist, was sentenced to die.[21]

The Gallows

It took months before Inspector Foelsche and the Post and Telegraph-Master John Little (who counted 'Deputy Sheriff' among his duties), plus a few troopers, boarded the specially chartered SS *Darwin* to take Wandy Wandy to Malay Bay for his execution. Once there, gallows were erected on the edge of a campground used often by the Iwaidja, and the clan gathered and waited.

Wandy Wandy also watched on, wearing heavy chains.

Then, on 25 July 1893, Wandy Wandy was forced to climb the gallows, and the noose was placed around his neck:

> … The drop was 6ft 6in, and death was instantaneous, not even a tremor or movement of the body of any kind occurring after the drop fell. Mr. Foelsche had collected about thirty natives who witnessed the execution. Three of these natives spoke English fluently and had been witnesses at the trial of Wandy Wandy. The body was left hanging for twenty minutes and was then cut down and buried at the place of execution. The gallows was left standing as a warning to natives, Malays, and others.[22]

Endnotes

1. aka Wandy Wandy.
2. In Searcy, 1909.
3. *NTTGG*, 14 May 1881, page 2: Law Courts. Circuit Court—Palmerston. Tuesday, 10th May. 1881
4. *NTTGG*, 21 August 1880, page 2: Police Court.
5. *NTTGG*, 23 March 1889, page 2: Served his Time.
6. "Marege" meant the "Wild Country" east from the Cobourg Peninsula as far as Groote Eylandt in the Gulf of Carpentaria
7. Other sources suggest the trade was much earlier, perhaps as far back as the 1500s (Rogers, 2014).
8. Searcy said they were 'strangers' blown down from the Aru Islands. Speaking a different dialect of Malay, they may not have been able to communicate well with the clan.
9. Searcy was quite capable of inventing stories – and often did to suit his audience in 1905. Mangerippy's story could be one of those, and though it is quoted here, it should be noted that it is a very smooth translation, and Searcy's work may not be historically correct.
10. This is probably Goose Lagoon, which unfortunately, is now a salt flat after feral buffalo tracks breached the sand dunes and allowed salt water intrusion.
11. Searcy, 1905, Page 41.
12. Searcy, 1905, page 41.
13. *NTTGG*, 18 November 1892, page 3: Law Courts, Police Court.
14. *NTTGG*, 18 November 1892 page 3: Law Courts, Police Court.
15. *NTTGG*, 13 November 1892. Only six men are mentioned here, though eight were to stand trial.
16. The jurors were Messrs. V. V. Brown, S. Budgen, G. McKeddie, M. D. Armstrong, A. A. Lewis, H. W. H. Stevens, S. T. Brown, R. R. Rundle, P. R. Freer, H. M. Debross, D. Daniels, and G. W. Mayhew.
17. *NTTGG*, 17 February 1893, page 3: Law Courts, Circuit Court –Palmerston.
18. *NTTGG*, 17 February 1893, page 3: Law Courts, Circuit Court –Palmerston.
19. *NTTGG*, 3 March 1893, page 2: Editorial.
20. *NTTGG*, 3 March 1893, page 2: Editorial.
21. Pressure to carry out the execution came from Premier Sir John Downer, QC, in Adelaide, *NTTGG*, 11 August 1893.
22. *NTTGG*, 11 August 1893, Page 2: The Hanging of Wandy Wandy.

Hanged: Execution in the Top End

Chapter 3
Moolooloorun, 1895

Hanged at Mole Hill on 17 January 1895, near the Roper River, for the murder of an unnamed Chinese man.

Figure 6: Robert Stott (c 1900, SLSA, B-39124).

In 1894, Mounted Constable Robert Stott was stationed at the Roper River Police Station. A future Commissioner of Central Australian Police, Stott had already been in the Roper River region for five years and knew most of the surrounding population by name. Attuned to any gossip that might amount to a lead, Stott listened when a tracker named Billy said he had heard there had been trouble at Mole Hill, some 70 km to the west, along the track towards Katherine. He immediately saddled his horse and set off to investigate. "I went to a flat three miles east of Mole Hill on the 8th of July," he said in the Circuit Court the next year:

> ... I saw signs of a struggle and the grass was all beaten down and smeared with something that looked like blood; I followed a path which went from this place about 20 yards to the north; it led me off the road, and I saw the remains of a Chinaman,

the body was lying on its back, head to the north; the legs and arms had been partly eaten away by wild dogs, and the body was much decomposed, looking as if dead about three weeks; the fore part of the skull was all broken in, and there was a crack from the base of the skull right down; I brought the skull to Palmerston, and handed it over to Dr. O'Flaherty for examination; I afterwards found another spot where there appeared to have been a struggle, about five or six yards north-west from the first place; the grass there was all tumbled down and smeared over with what appeared to me to be blood; I was unable to find any tracks leading from the latter place; the grass in the locality is very high and very thick... [1]

The Victims

The victim was one of two Chinese men who had been travelling through Mole Hill.

Even today this a remote part of the Territory. A highway travels east-west between Elsey Station on the Stuart Highway and Leichhardt's Bar and then crosses the river on a recently built all-weather bridge before it reaches the communities of Ngukurr and, further on, Numbulwar. At Leichhardt's Bar (aka Roper Bar) an unsealed road splits off and heads along the river, eventually turning south to reach the Heartbreak Hotel at Cape Crawford and through to Borroloola. These roads roughly follow the tracks that were created and used for millennia by the Indigenous clans of the area, but first used by non-Aboriginal travelers in the 1870s.

Leichhardt's Bar is an important crossing point of the Roper River. Just downstream, a supply depot for the Overland Telegraph Line construction parties was established because the 80 km stretch of river from the river mouth is navigable by ships. To reach the depot by land, a track for bullock drays and horse carts was established for use throughout the dry season. In the wet, vehicles could easily become bogged in creek crossings, or quagmires. The Bar was an obvious place to build facilities for local bushmen and travelers, and a store was established nearby by William Hay in 1885. The police station

Chapter 3: Moolooloorun 1895

came soon after,[2] because the bar was the only place to cross the river for many miles, and the police could keep an eye on it and the entire area from there. The Roper River Police Station existed from 1885 until its transfer to Ngukurr in 1982 and M.C. Robert Stott[3] was part of a long line of outback policemen to be stationed there.

Given the remoteness of the track, who were the murder victims? What were two Chinese travelers doing there on foot? Where were they going?

Anti-Chinese sentiment reached a fever-pitch across much of Australia in the 1890s. Large numbers of Chinese men (and some women) had come to the Territory following the alluvial gold rush of the 1870s, and work in the 1880s. The work ranged from railway construction on the Palmerston to Pine Creek line, to mining in underground mines on the tribute system (paying 10-15% of gold won to an 'employer'), and many Chinese people also became storekeepers, market gardeners, tailors, servants, fishermen and cooks on the cattle stations.

The anti-Chinese feelings of the other Australian colonies were less obvious in the Top End. The Northern Territory needed workers and in 1891, Chinese people outnumbered Europeans in the Territory by three to one. Some Europeans were afraid of being swamped, but nevertheless, Darwin businessmen petitioned the South Australian Government seeking to reverse their anti-Chinese policies. They needed cheap labour. For the Chinese, however, the Territory was not as inviting as the Europeans seemed to think it was. New people still arrived, but many Chinese chose to go home to China rather than struggle in the Australian bush. In 1894 there were 3,566 Chinese residents counted in the Territory, with 2,015 of them engaged in mining.[4] There were just 891 Europeans[5] but they, despite being a quarter of the population of the former, ran most of the businesses, owned almost all the mines, worked in the administration, kept the records, wrote the laws, published the newspapers, and governed.

Deciding the 'grass to be greener on the other side of the

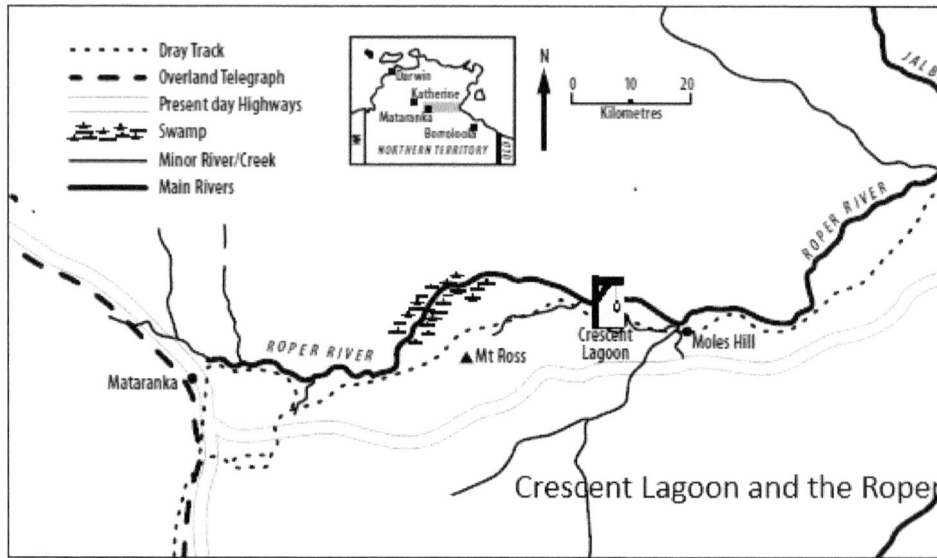

Crescent Lagoon and the Roper

fence,' Queensland became a more attractive proposition for many disillusioned Chinese men. The problem was getting there – and the cost. Queensland imposed a £10 poll tax on all Chinese people who landed in their ports and this, added to transport fares, was too much.

Walking was their only option. It was a 1500 km overland trek from Palmerston to Camooweal, just over the border, but once there the travelers could look for work on the cattle stations or in the mines north of Cairns. Unknown numbers went this way. The overland trail passed through Katherine, turned east at the Roper River, and worked its way to the Queensland border. Not all travelers were successful. Some died of thirst, others were no doubt killed by locals and their bodies never discovered, and others were arrested in Queensland on their arrival:

> ... a number of Chinese were crossing the border at the extreme north-western boundary into Queensland with a view of evading the poll tax. The police were at once set to work, and succeeded in arresting six Chinamen at Camooweal, a township about 200 miles from Cloncurry... The border between Urandangie and Camooweal is being carefully patrolled, and it is anticipated that several other arrests will be made.[6]

Chapter 3: Moolooloorun 1895

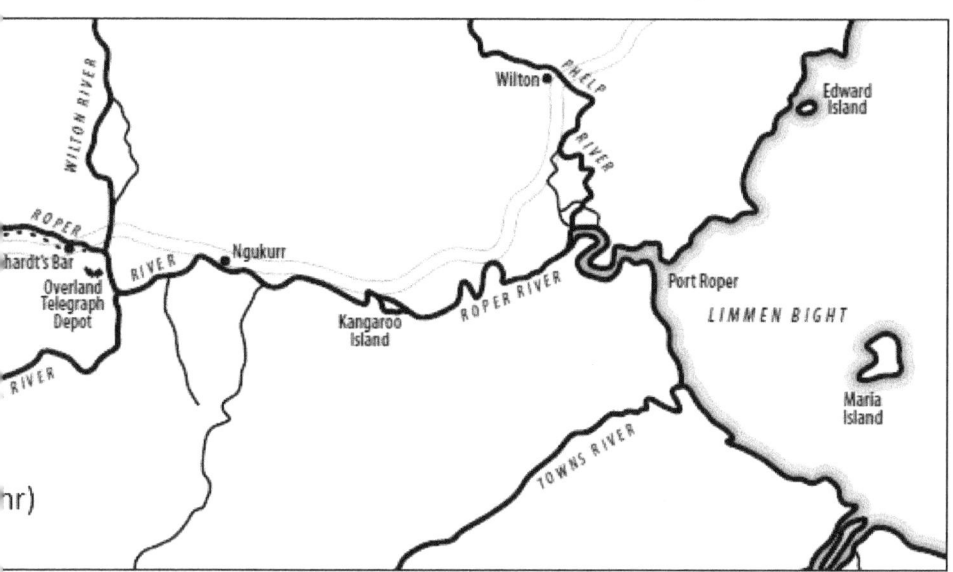

Map 3: Crescent Lagoon was on the track between Elsey Station and the Leichhardt Bar on the Roper River. Moolooloorun was hanged here, in front of his clan, on 17 January 1895 (Map courtesy of Frank Uhr.)

Figure 7: Emphasising the danger of travelling the overland trail, this traveller died at the base of this overland telegraph pole, possibly of thirst (SLSA, PRG-280-1-16, 1914).

Mounted Constable Stretton, stationed at the McArthur River Police Station, reported 40 Chinese travelers in just a few months in 1893. He was worried that the Queensland unionists would force them to return to the Territory, and indeed, many were turned back. Sixty-six Chinese were arrested at the border that year and expelled, only to try again in small groups at different places along the border. Eleven of them were re-arrested, but of the other 55 there has never been any word.[7]

So, the two Chinese travelers attacked and killed near Mole Hill in July 1894 were probably two of many dozens of Chinese men to make the journey that year. Unfortunately for them, they were at the wrong place at the wrong time.

The Killers

A police tracker named Billy told Mounted Constable Stott that two local men, Moolooloorun and Nyanko, had killed the Chinese travellers to rob them of their tobacco. Immediately ready for a patrol, Stott mounted up and easily tracked down Nyanko in his camp, arresting him on 13 July.

Nyanko spoke English and Stott put his story down in writing: "Me killem" he said, "along here (patting the back of head)"

> ... Moolooloorun and me; sleep one fellow night along Mole Hill; go back along Chinaman; one fellow Chinaman been run away along bush; me blanket, mosquito net, and one fellow tobacco; Moolooloorun one blanket, shirt, tobacco, money plenty."[8]

A few days later, while Stott prepared to transfer Nyanko to Palmerston via the Pine Creek railway, they visited the site of the murder. Nyanko seemed happy to point out where his victim had lain.

> ... he pointed to it and said, " This man dead"; he then went to the other place and said, "This one run away along bush."[9]

Stott had known Moolooloorun for five years, so he too was easy to find. On 27 July he was arrested about three miles west of

Chapter 3: Moolooloorun 1895

Crescent Lagoon:

> ... I told him the charge, and I cautioned him; he speaks English... he made a statement to me, as follows —"Tommy and Jimmy him too much talk along me; me two fellow bin follow Chinaman and killem along road."[10]

Moolooloorun and Nyanko's confessions to M.C. Stott were surprisingly frank. They had seen the tracks of two Chinese men and followed them along the road to catch up with them:

> ... me two fellow bin follow Chinaman and killem along road... This blanket and calico belong to me; I bin catchem along dead fellow Chinaman; this one blanket ... bin take from Chinaman that go bush; I bin take dead fellow Chinaman's stick, Nyanko bin take stick from Chinaman that go along bush; two fellow stick sit down along river; Chinaman along bush no more got tucker and blanket; him walk nothing; Chinaman bin too much finish tucker, only a little me bin tobacco me get 'em like that (3 sticks); Nyanko all the same; black-fellow too much talk; me and Nyanko follow Chinaman's track; he kill 'em a little bit on the ground – Nyanko bin kill him the side of the head: two fellow Chinamen been tumble down and me run away frightened; me one fellow sleep; plenty blacks go back along Chinaman; me and Nyanko pull dead Chinaman along bush.[11]

Moolooloorun had cut a stick to use as a weapon if he was refused the tobacco he wanted, and he had used it to hit one of the Chinese men and crush his skull. Nyanko hit the other on the back of the head but, although the man fell, he managed to get back on his feet and run into the bush. He was never seen again and Nyanko believed he had died, though he had never seen the body. The victims' belongings (blankets, calico, mosquito net, and a few sticks of tobacco) were then gathered up and kept, although their clothes were burned the next day.

Moolooloorun was a leader among his clan with the reputation of being their rainmaker. His age is unrecorded but as a senior member of his clan he was probably already considered an elder. Nyanko was a young man who was perhaps easily led – would that make a difference at the trial?

The Circuit Court

The Circuit Court was ready on 7 August 1894, and Justice Dashwood and the jury settled in to listen to the facts and make their judgement.

One witness was missing. The tracker named Billy could not be called because he was dead. His readiness to report the killing may have angered someone in his clan because when M.C. Stott passed Red Lily Swamp on 14 July, Billy was still alive but showed Stott a wound on the side of his head. He died of infection four days later, so was no longer around to attend the trial. Billy's information, however, allowed Stott to gather other witness who could attest that the murderers had boasted of their deed at a corroboree near Elsey River. Chief among them was an elder named Jimmy. Jimmy knew the offenders well, and he was the first to give a testimony at the trial:

> I heard the prisoner Moolooloorun talk at the corroboree; he said he saw tracks at Mole Hill and following them saw Chinamen along the road; then he said he cut stick all-the-same nulla and went back to the Chinese and asked them for tobacco, which they would not give him; Mooloolarun [sic] said he then hit the Chinaman with the nulla nulla, and the Chinaman fell down and then the other prisoner (Nyanko) said he had killed another Chinaman by hitting him on the back of the head; the Chinaman fell down on the grass close up to the road; but he afterwards got up and went away into the bush.
>
> Nyanko told me he had killed a Chinaman; the prisoners then took, blankets, calico, mosquito net, and a few sticks tobacco; Davy, Jimmy, Tommy, and the prisoners then pulled the Chinamen through the grass; they then went to the river and slept, and next day went back to for the Chinamen, but found only one there; the blacks agreed to leave the other body in the grass; Jimmy took the Chinaman's clothes to the camp and burnt them: I saw the pannikin produced in court, Moolooloorun had it; when he showed it he said he had killed a Chinaman; I asked him what he killed the Chinaman for,

and he growled at me; I told the blackfellow Billy to go and tell the Roper policeman; the Mole Hill blacks knew that I sent Billy to the Roper.[12]

Dr O'Flaherty assured the jury that there had indeed been a killing – he had the skull of the victim to prove it:

> I examined on 5th inst. a skull brought to me by M. C. Stott; the skull had portions of scalp adherent, also a queue, which with other characteristics proved it to be that of a Chinaman; the lower jaw was with the portion of skull; the right lateral and lateral portion of the skull were broken; there was also a fracture running up left side in direction from base to crown; the bones of face were broken front angle of orbits downwards; didn't notice any teeth in the skull: should say the damage was caused by blunt instrument — such as a waddy or heavy stick; did not notice any marks of a sharp instrument; should say the body to which the skull belonged had been dead over a month.[13]

In defending the men, Counsellor Symes suggested that their confessions were inadmissible and should be thrown out because "of the improper way in which the caution had been administered to the prisoners."[14]

> … It was hardly the style of caution that one would give a blackfellow in so serious a matter. Prisoner might have taken it for anything, even for an invite to tell his story candidly, so that Mr. Stott might "yabber along plenty whitefellow" in Palmerston.[15]

Justice Dashwood agreed that there might be an issue with them, but he "would not veto the evidence of the constable," and he allowed the confessions on their face value.

The court listened to the evidence for almost a whole day. Late in the afternoon, the jury retired, but they took only a few minutes to consider and return with their verdict. Moolooloorun and Nyanko were guilty, and Justice Dashwood took no time in sentencing both to death 'in the usual manner.' Now condemned, the prisoners were returned in chains to the cells in Fannie Bay Gaol to await the gallows.

Five months later the Executive Council met in Adelaide

Hanged: Execution in the Top End

to discuss the sentences. Their decision was soon telegraphed to Palmerston:

> An intimation has been received from the Government Resident's Office to the effect that the supreme authorities at Adelaide have come to a final decision in the matter of the two aboriginals, Nyanko and Moolooloorun, who, at the Circuit Court in August last, were found guilty of the murder of a Chinaman near the Roper River and were sentenced to death by Mr. Justice Dashwood. It has been decided that in the case of the younger prisoner, Nyanko, his sentence shall be commuted to imprisonment for life, but that in reference to the other the law must take its course. The date for the execution of Moolooloorun has been fixed as the 17th of January, and arrangements are being made to hang him at Crescent Lagoon, which is situated about nine miles from the scene of the murder.[16]

It was not before time, commented the *Times* in the *Notes of the Week* column. They thought that waiting on death row for six months was cruel punishment:

> … If there is no other satisfaction to be derived from the purposed hanging of the blackfellow Moolooloorun it will at least wipe out for the time being that ghastly blemish on our constitution of keeping a prisoner waiting six months for his fate. This blackfellow was sentenced to death on the 8th of August, and he has been ironed in gaol ever since. Within a week of his sentence, he was probably forgotten by everyone but his gaolers, and there was never the slightest intention on the part of anyone to appeal on his behalf. At his trial he was practically self-convicted, and when a prisoner confesses his guilt, all avenues leading to an appeal may

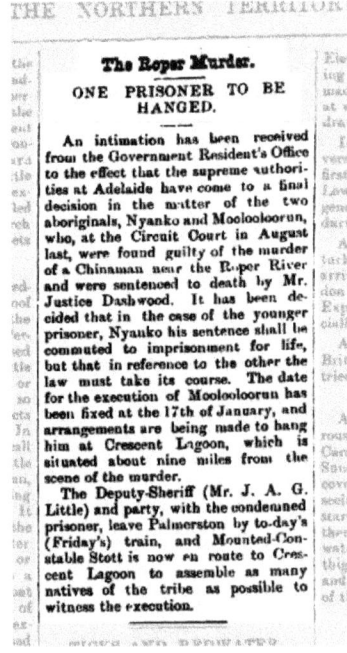

Figure 8: *Northern Territory Times and Government Gazette*, 28 Dec 1894, page 3.

be considered to be blocked. In such a case if hanging is to be done at last it seems harsh and unmerciful to keep the doomed man manacled in prison for half a year waiting to know what the white man proposes to do with him next. Serious persons who have had much experience of our courts know that the average trial of natives is a weird farce. The conventional forms and ceremonies are carried out with care and precision, but for all that the native knows about them the court might just as well be dealing with a block of wood. The farce is not ended until the wretched creatures are made to wait six months for the final act. Is it not time that we made an earnest endeavour to introduce a system with less of an air of brutality about it?[17]

Crescent Lagoon

In keeping with the policy of executing Aboriginal people where the murders had occurred – as Wandy Wandy had been two years before – once the date was decided, the government had just 20 days to organise the execution. Crescent Lagoon lies east of Mataranka, separated, but not far from, the Roper River. Almost forgotten today, the Lagoon was a regular camping spot for travellers on the dray track to the Overland Telegraph Line Depot at Roper Bar and an important meeting site for the local Aboriginal clans.

It had seen trouble before. In 1875, a telegraph operator named Charles Johnston had been speared and killed near Roper Bar,[18] and several retribution parties went out to "disperse the natives". The first, a party of nine men led by George De Latour and William Batten, was soon followed by a police party led by Corporal Montague, with orders from Inspector Foelsche to "have a picnic with the natives."[19] A civilian group arrived about the same time. Funded and armed by the government, it was led by Johnston's brother-in-law, none other than telegraph superintendent and future deputy sheriff, John Little.

Researchers have identified no less than five massacres of Aboriginal people by these retribution posses along this stretch of river, including at Crescent Lagoon.[20]

As Tony Roberts recorded:

... an overlanding party led by George De Lautour (a man of dubious character), *en route* to Queensland, found the note and slaughtered an unknown number of people at Mole Hill before burning their huts and weapons. When the official party of police and civilians arrived at Roper Bar on 2 August, they found letters dated 19 and 24 July from one of De Lautour's (sic: De Latour] men describing the punishment delivered. They also visited the remains of the Aboriginal camp and saw the dead bodies. A member of the official party later wrote that the overlanders "dispersed them thoroughly ... [and] fully avenged Johnston's death"[21]

After this, the official party set to work slaughtering Aboriginals on both sides of the river upstream from Roper Bar. On 20 August, police reinforcements arrived on a government boat from Darwin and the slaughter continued downstream from the Bar, as far as the river mouth, notwithstanding that those tribes had nothing to do with Johnston's murder. The random killings extended along a 200 kilometre stretch that ran both north and south of the river.

When the boat departed, the land party returned to Mole Hill where, on 4 September, they shot more people. The total death toll is impossible to guess but was likely in excess of 150 or 200.[22]

Twenty years later, John Little returned to Crescent Lagoon as the deputy sheriff, tasked with ensuring the death of one more Aboriginal man from that region. This time, of course, it was legal.

The 300-mile journey to Crescent Lagoon could be made by railway as far as Pine Creek, but the rest required horses and horse carts. It was not an easy journey, made worse by the weather, for January lies in the Top End's wet season, when the roads can be quagmires and the rivers can rise rapidly. It cannot have been a comfortable trip for a man in chains.

On Friday 28 December, almost three weeks before the assigned date for the execution, Little, Sergeant Waters and their party, climbed on board the waiting carriage at Palmerston Railway Station. Moolooloorun, weighed down by his chains, was heading back to his country. His emotions went unrecorded, of course, but perhaps he viewed this as an unexpected kindness that he was thankful for.

The Gallows

Mounted Constable Stott had gone ahead a few days earlier to get to Crescent Lagoon in time to "assemble as many natives of the tribe as possible to witness the execution" and by the time Little and Moolooloorun arrived, he had managed to gather 59 of the condemned man's countrymen.

Then, on a steamy wet-season morning, on the peaceful banks of the lagoon, Moolooloorun was duly hanged in front of them. It was 17 January 1895, just over six months since the murder.

Moolooloorun's death was instantaneous and "not especially interesting."[23] As for his family and countrymen – how they felt can only be guessed at, but it seemed to the white officials that there was "no sign of alarm at this, to them, strange manner of taking life."[24]

The editor of the *Times*, kept his sympathy for John Little:

> … No doubt the Deputy-Sheriff feels more contented in mind now than he had done for a week or two previous to the execution. There is no comfort to be derived from a duty which compels you to travel a journey of 300 miles with a murderer in tow for the purpose of hanging the convicted one at a specified time on a specified date; and in wet weather, too, when annoying delays might occur any day. Then, besides weather conditions, there was also the possibility, a vague one, perhaps, of the prisoner escaping, or of the hangman deserting. As, however, none of these disasters overtook the party, and as the convict was executed in the most approved style, the Deputy-Sheriff should return to his headquarters in a fine state of mental complacency after his 600-mile journey.[25]

The Chinese victim's body, minus his head, remains buried in a forgotten grave, near where he was found on the track between Crescent Lagoon and Mole Hill. He is unnamed and unclaimed, as his identity was never discovered.

No one knows what happened to his skull after the court was finished with it.

Endnotes

1. *NTTGG*, 10 August 1894, page 3: Circuit Court.
2. There are references to police stationed at nearby Mount McMinn in 1884. Corporal Power was named as the OIC by Alfred Searcy in In Australian Tropics (Searcy, 1909).
3. Robert Stott served at Southport, Roper Bar, Burrundie, Katherine, Borroloola, was sergeant of the Mounted Police in Alice Springs, and then Commissioner of Police, Centralian Police Force. He was killed after being hit by a train in 1928, aged 70 (Kimber, 1990).
4. Charles Dashwood, Government Resident's Report for the Year 1894 (LANT).
5. Jones, 1990.
6. *Telegraph*, Monday 27 July 1891, page 2: Evading the Poll Tax.
7. Jones, 1990.
8. *NTTGG*, 10 August 1894, page 3: Circuit Court.
9. *NTTGG*, 10 August 1894, page 3: Circuit Court
10. *NTTGG*, 10 August 1894, page 3: Circuit Court
11. *NTTGG*, 10 August 1894, page 3: Circuit Court
12. *NTTGG*, 10 August 1894, page 3: Circuit Court
13. *NTTGG*, 10 August 1894, page 3: Circuit Court
14. *NTTGG*, 10 August 1894, page 3: Circuit Court
15. *NTTGG*, 10 August 1894, page 3: Circuit Court
16. *NTTGG*, 28 December 1894, page 3: The Roper Murder: One Prisoner to be Hanged, and Daily Telegraph, 13 December 1894, page 5 Commutation of a Death Sentence.
17. *NTTGG*, 28 December 1894, page 2: Notes of the Week.
18. See Pugh 2022.
19. Reid 1990.
20. Smith, 2024.
21. *NTTGG*, 18 August 1875.
22. Roberts 2009.
23. *NTTGG*, 1 February 1895, page 3: Notes of the Week.
24. *NTTGG*, 1 February 1895, page 3: Notes of the Week.
25. *NTTGG*, 25 January 1895, page 2: Notes of the Week.

Chapter 4
Chung Yeung and Lem Kai, 1899

Hanged in Fannie Bay Gaol on 10 August 1899, for the murder of Chee Hang at Yam Creek.

The killers were a part of a Chinese population living on and around the goldfields some 160 km from Palmerston. Yam Creek, the earliest of the goldrush settlements, at one time had a hotel, police station, and telegraph station, but these had long gone – moved down the track to the town of Burrundie. Nevertheless, tents and humpies still dotted the countryside and, according to the Government Resident's Report for 1899, there were still 80 Chinese miners seeking ever more of its hidden treasures at Yam Creek.[1] As this was half the number of two years earlier, abandoned huts were common. They were made of bush timber, bark and grass, and often strengthened with the flattened tin from flour drums or corrugated iron. Remnants of rusty metal are still spread throughout the goldfields, but the bush has long since reclaimed the rest.

The Victim

Chee Hang lived in one of these huts. Hang's hut was probably no different to the others, and he was probably just one of the crowd. Nothing is known about him, except that he was apparently arguing with two of his neighbours. Chee claimed Chung Yeung[2] and Lem

Figure 9: Chinese miner's hut at Pine Creek (1923, SLSA, B-23036).

Kai had stolen some gold from him and in return, Yeung had been heard blaming Chee Hang for stealing rations from his hut.

Numerous people had heard Chung threaten to shoot Chee Hang with his gun and burn his body[3] and this may be exactly what he did.

One day in August 1898, Chee Hang's friends noticed that he was missing and set out to look for him. They came across Lem Kai and Chung Yeung scattering the remains of a fire with shovels and while this may not have been unusual, they became suspicious when the pair fled. Examining the fire, they found what looked like human remains among the ashes. They were right – the remains were later identified by Doctor Collins as "the heart and part of the jaw and fingers of a human being."[4]

The police were called. The argument between Chee Hang and Chung Yeung had apparently turned violent and Chung was accused of fatally shooting Chee when he was fishing at a billabong near his garden.

With the help of the Chinese community, the police soon tracked down both Lem Kai and Chung Yeung. Unfortunately for them, the alleged killers found no support at all from their compatriots. They believed that Kai and Yeung lived by thieving, and no one was surprised that they were in trouble. Some might have been relieved that they had been locked up.

The following March they were defended by the future Government Resident, Charles Herbert, in a trial that turned out to take an unusually long time for the era, especially since they both confessed. It lasted "all through Tuesday, and up to 11.15 on Wednesday night…"[5]

> … Both prisoners confessed to the crime at their trial, the only disparity being that one said he shot him with a revolver, and the other stated that a shot gun was used. Having killed the unfortunate Celestial, the two men cooked the body and chopped it up with an axe to prevent identification.[6]

Chung Yeung and Lem Kai were clearly guilty, with Yeung having been the shooter. What made the murder particularly abhorrent was their action in chopping up and cooking the body afterwards. The *Adelaide Observer* described their crime as "one of the most diabolical [murders] ever perpetrated in the colonies."[7]

The victim was unrecognisable, "so completely did they carry out their gruesome task that not one bone was left unbroken, and only the heart remained intact."[8]

The murder of Chee Hang may not have been the only killing conducted by these two, because another Chinese man had been found burned to death in his hut about the same time. These huts were partly made of grass, so the authorities had concluded that the man had fallen asleep with a burning opium pipe, and that the fire was accidental. But members of the Chinese community thought otherwise, and accused Chung Yeung and Lem Kai of the man's murder. This, though, was never brought to trial.

> **A NORTHERN TERRITORY TRAGEDY.**
>
> **MURDER OF A CHINAMAN.**
>
> PORT DARWIN, Thursday.—This morning, at Faunie Bay Gaol, the death sentence passed on Lem Kai and Chung Yeung, two Chinamen, for the murder of Chee Yung, was carried out. Both of the prisoners admitted their guilt to Tear Jack, a Chinese missionary, who attended them before execution, and they went to their death with stoical demeanor. The executioner and his assistant were prisoners in the gaol. Death was instantaneous.
>
> In July, 1898, a Chinaman, Chee Hung, living at Yam Creek, disappeared, and a few days afterwards certain human bones were discovered in Chung Yung's garden, and near the hut occupied by Lem Kai and Chung Yeung. An official inquiry was made, which resulted in the arrest of the two Chinamen, who were tried for murder at the Circuit Court in March last. The circumstantial evidence was so strong that the jury found both prisoners guilty of wilful murder. The evidence showed that neither of the prisoners ever did any work, and apparently lived by thieving. Some time previous to the murder of Chee Hung, another Chinaman was found burnt to death in his hut, and at the time it was supposed that deceased, being addicted to the opium habit, had gone to sleep, and that his bed had caught fire accidentally. The Chinese residents say that Kai and Yeung also killed this man from motives of robbery. The Chinese community is well satisfied with the death penalty, which they consider richly deserved.

Figure 10: *Daily Telegraph*, 11 August 1899, page 6, with variations to the story told by others.

The Circuit Court

TUESDAY, MARCH 21, 1899.

Before His Honor Mr. Justice Dashwood…[9] Lem Kai and Chung Yeung, two Chinese, were charged that they did in July last, at Yam Creek, kill and afterwards burn one Chinaman named Chung Lung.

Sergeant Waters conducted the case for the prosecution.

Mr. Herbert appeared on behalf of the prisoners.

The evidence in this case took up the time of the Court all through Tuesday, and up to 11.15 on Wednesday night, and was far too voluminous to allow our publishing fully.[10]

The Jury found the prisoners guilty of willful murder, and they were sentenced to death, His Honor holding out no hope of mercy.[11]

Dashwood's decision not to offer the condemned any hope of mercy meant that their sentence of death by hanging would never be commuted to a lesser penalty. They had four months of confinement to endure, and then they would be led to the gallows.

Condemned, and despised by the Chinese community, the media were happy to report that their compatriots were "well satisfied with the death penalty, which they consider richly deserved."[12]

Finding a hangman was a problem, and rumours were rife about who it was going to be. They were so contagious that the *Times* felt it necessary to deny some of them:

> … there is no truth in the rumour that Ryland is to be the executioner.[13]

Poor George Ryland[14], publican of the Rum Jungle Hotel, must have been receiving unwarranted attention. The *Times* was also keen to help:

> Wanted, a hangman! Inquisitive ones are already wondering who will give the "drop too much" to the prisoners under sentence of death in Fanny[15] Bay Gaol… two at least are sure to get off, but the two Chinese… These miscreants fully deserve the hangman's rope, and the lesson may not be lost on our Asiatic community which badly wants keeping in check.[16]

The Gallows

Gaoler George Norcock pointed out that the gallows last used in Flannigan's execution in 1893 were no longer fit for purpose in 1899. They were second-hand when they had arrived in Palmerston in 1886, and they had been erected and dismantled so many times that the coverboards were loose, and the whole structure was shaky. Plus:

> … the white ants went through the centre of the uprights, causing it to be still more unreliable and shows that the uprights must be of iron or built on a concrete foundation.

Norcock requested permanent gallows to be built within the prison yard:

> … with all the latest improvements to levers etc, and sufficiently strong to hang three at once.[17]

In the end, it seems the old gallows were patched up and again pressed into service, and permanent gallows were not installed until half a century had passed.

A hangman was found in Deputy Sheriff John Little's usual way. He recruited a prisoner from the gaol willing to do the deed in exchange for an early release.

The biggest issue on the day of the hanging was the worry that it might clash with the races. The *Times* was quick to alleviate any concerns, however, in a callous, pun-filled note:

> The annual races of the NTRC commence today. Five minutes' walk from the course the two Chinese murderers are to be hanged. But the two things won't clash, as the convicts will 'drop' early in the morning, whereas the sporting fraternity won't have a chance to 'drop' on the races till 12.30. Those who witness the hanging will be able to step a few paces across the road and get all thoughts of it out of their heads by plunging on the tote.[18]

And quietly, without drawing too much attention to the gaol, Chung Yeung and Lem Kai were led to the gallows. The *Northern Territory Times* failed to name them, but told its readers that:

> The two Chinese sentenced to death for the murder and subsequent burning of a countryman, were hanged at Fanny Bay Prison on Thursday morning last. Only a very few officials and invited persons witnessed the execution.
>
> The condemned men were attended by the Rev. Mr. Tear Tack, Wesleyan Missionary preacher, who states that they expressed great contrition for their sin.
>
> Both walked firmly to the scaffold, and when the bolt was drawn the two bodies dropped like a flash, and death was instantaneous in each case.
>
> After the customary lapse of time the bodies were cut down and buried in the prison cemetery.[19]

The news was quickly telegraphed around Australia, and many regional newspapers found room for the story. Like the *Coolgardie Miner* (see figure 11), most newspapers were reasonably respectful, correctly naming the executed men and barely changing the telegraphed text.

Chapter 4: Chung Yeung and Lem Kai, 1899

Others gave little more than three of four lines of their columns, and at least one made no attempt to hide the paper's racist leanings. They simply chose the heading "Two Chows Less."

Figure 11: *Coolgardie Miner*, 11 August 1899.

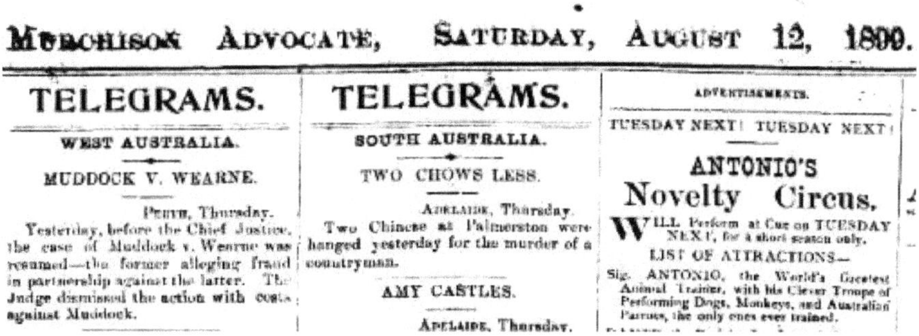

Figure 12: "Two Chows Less" (*Murchison Advocate*, 12 August 1899, page 3).

Endnotes

1. Jones, 1990
2. Aka Chung Young.
3. *NTTGG*, 12 August 1898, page 3: Murder at Yam Creek.
4. *NTTGG*, 12 August 1898, page 3: Murder at Yam Creek.
5. *NTTGG*, 24 March 1899, page 3: Palmerston Circuit Court.
6. *Adelaide Observer*, 5 August 1899, page 14: The Northern Territory Murders.
7. *Adelaide Observer*, 5 August 1899, page 14: The Northern Territory Murders.
8. *Adelaide Observer*, 5 August 1899, page 14: The Northern Territory Murders.
9. The jury consisted of Messrs. H. Adcock (foreman), H. Pinder, J. Shanahan, C. Witherden, H.A.G. Rundle, W. Taylor, M. Myles, J. Roberts, F. Whiteford, and A. Pott. None of them were Chinese.
10. Most trials of interest at the time were thoroughly documented, often with transcripts of the proceedings appearing in the Times. Unfortunately, the transcripts of this trial were not printed, and archival searches have been unsuccessful, so those verbatim records appear to be lost.
11. *NTTGG*, 24 March 1899, page 3: Palmerston Circuit Court.
12. Singleton Argus, 12 August 1899.
13. *NTTGG*, 11 August 1899, page 2: Notes of the Week.
14. Note, this is George Henry Ryland (1844-1911), not George Ryland (1855-1920) the Director of Lands and Water Supply, after whom Ryland Road is named. This later George arrived in Darwin in 1912.
15. Fanny Bay is now universally called Fannie Bay.
16. *NTTGG*, 31 March 1899: Notes of the Week.
17. Norcott to Little, 25 April 1899: copy of correspondence in Dewar 1981 ex Barbara James.
18. *NTTGG*, 11 August 1899, page 2: Notes of the Week.
19. *NTTGG*, 18 August 1899, page 3: Execution at Fanny Bay [sic]. The cemetery was in the grounds of the gaol, but its exact location has been lost.

Chapter 5
Jimmy, 1901

Hanged at Shaws Creek on 8 April 1901, for the murder of John Larson.

The Victims

In mid-July 1900, rumours spread like wildfire across the tiny community of Palmerston. News had come in via Brocks Creek of a mutiny off the western coast. The kerosene powered launch *Wunwulla*, belonging to Captain Joe Bradshaw, had been overtaken, the rumours said, by the Aboriginal crew and the white men on board were all dead.

The crew were well known. There was John (Jack) Larson and Engineer Ivan Egeroff,[1] and an Aboriginal crew of three: Jimmy, George (aka Josie) and a 12-year-old boy named Georgie.

The *Wunwulla* had left Port Darwin the week before in company with the sailing yacht *Minniehaha*, under Captain Mugg, and it had arrived at the Daly River mouth and moored for the night. Also on board were a couple of Daly River men, named Cockatoo and Fennem, whom Larson had employed as pilots to guide them up the river.

Arriving under sail the next day, Captain Mugg spotted *Wunwulla's* dinghy in the Daly River. It was drifting in the tide without oars, helpless, and within it sat Ivan Egeroff, very much alive. Ivan told Mugg that he had been asleep in the *Wunwulla* when he had been suddenly attacked and thrown overboard.

Mugg immediately sent the news of the mutiny via a "black runner" to Harry Neimann,[2] at the Daly River Mission, and Neimann passed the letter on to Brocks Creek, three day's travel away, because there was access to both the railway and the telegraph in the little mining town. In Brocks Creek, a butcher named William Byrne wired the police in Palmerston on Thursday morning, 19 July – a week after the mutiny:

> When Captain Mugg arrived at the mouth of the Daly River he picked up Ivan (Mr. Bradshaw's engineer) in a dingey [sic] without paddles. Ivan told Mugg that he had been thrown out of the launch by a Victoria River blackboy; he managed to catch hold of the dingey which was towing after, but he had scarcely got into it when the painter was cut, and he drifted away. The flood tide was strong at the time, and he succeeded in getting the boat into the mangroves by paddling with his hands, where Mugg found him. He also told Mugg that as he was drifting away, he heard the sound of a shot and cries.
>
> In going up the river Mugg's boat got stranded at the Horseshoe Bend, and to avoid delay he dispatched some blacks to Mr. Niemann with a letter to be forwarded to nearest station and reported to the police and Mr. Bradshaw. Mr. Niemann sent the letter in to me, and I reported the matter to Inspector Foelsche and Mr. Bradshaw and also wired the whole contents of the letter to the Government Resident.
>
> The messengers (two blackboys) were dispatched by Mr. Niemann after the moon rose on Saturday night and reached Brocks Creek (30 miles) by 4 o'clock on Monday afternoon, travelling on foot. Since then, no further news has come to hand, but Mr. Niemann promises to send in a messenger at once should the launch turn up.[3]

The story was more complete when Byrne followed up with a second letter that arrived from Harry Niemann that afternoon:

> Dear Mr. Byrne, we are now able to supply fuller details about Mr. Bradshaw's launch, Ivan having arrived here. He talks of returning in the *Minniehaha* tomorrow but is very weak. He states that the launch arrived at mouth of river at sundown

Chapter 5: Jimmy, 1901

on 10th inst., and Larson went ashore for a black pilot, returning about 7 pm and shortly after turning in. Ivan stayed up watching the tide and noticed the blacks were awake and acting strangely, but they said they had fever, and he put it down to that.

About 1.30, after getting all ready for a start, and calling Larson, he was feeling the strain on the anchor chain when one of the Victoria River black boys hit him on the back of the head with something heavy, swearing at same time. He is sure it was the Victoria River blacks and not the Daly River boys, two of whom Larson had brought on board. The blow stunned him, and he was then thrown overboard. The water revived him, and as he rose to the surface, he heard Larson shouting to him to go into the dingey. He succeeded in doing so, but the painter was at once cut. He had no oars but tried to paddle back to the launch with the footboard. The tide was running strongly in, but he was making slow progress when one of the blacks fired at him with a rifle, the ball striking the water close to the boat. He saw then that he had no chance of getting on board alive and allowed the boat to drift up stream until the tide was nearly full when he managed to reach the mangroves and get ashore after struggling through mud up to his waist. This was about 4 a.m. on Wednesday morning.

He rested till daybreak, when he got into the boat again and went out to see what had become of the launch. She was nowhere to be seen, and as Larson could not have got away against the tide until 4 a.m. he would scarcely have got out of sight before daylight and supposing he had got away, the *Minniehaha*, which was anchored at the Red Cliff, would almost certainly have seen the launch. Ivan states that he heard a second shot fired when he was drifting away, and as the blacks were between Larson and the firearms, he is very much afraid Larson has been murdered and the launch scuttled. If so, then either the Daly or the Victoria River blacks are in possession of rifles and cartridges, and Young and other station managers should be warned at once.

There is a rumour among the blacks here that the Daly blacks murdered the Victoria blacks and got all the plunder, but there is nothing definite and little reliance is to be placed on this. Ivan was carried out to sea by tide but was picked up by the

> *Minniehaha* at 2 p.m. on Wednesday, thoroughly exhausted from exposure to cold and wet.'
>
> As the *Minniehaha* was to leave the copper landing on Tuesday morning, she should be here today or tomorrow and may bring further news of the fate of the other man and the launch. Despite the fact of her not having been seen, it seems most probable that the launch has gone on to the Victoria River, as it is known that the Victoria River natives were quite capable of managing her. In that event it may be regarded as almost certain that Larson has been murdered.[4]

Mounted Constables Robert Stott and Fred Stone[5] immediately set off to investigate. And indeed, found that Larson was dead and the boat ransacked:

> After a search at the Daly River, the police found the launch in one of the creeks running into the river. Everything movable on board had been destroyed or carried away, and the launch was covered with broken materials, blood, and mud. The police came across four blacks and learned from them that the attack on the launch was not made by the two Daley [sic] River blacks, as previously reported, but by three Victoria River boys, part of the crew of the launch. It appears that these, after throwing the engineer overboard, seized Larson, the other white man, and while two of them held him, the third presented a rifle at his head.
>
> Larson cried out: "Don't! don't! What for kill me? I been good fellow 'long-a-you."
>
> The leader of the mutineers replied: "No matter; me kill you;" and immediately fired.
>
> The bullet passed through his right temple. They then threw his dead body into the river.[6]

Apparently, the Daly River men remonstrated with the mutineers and were then themselves attacked by tomahawks, but they jumped overboard and swam ashore. Jimmy and George had then taken the launch to where it was found, looted it, and headed off towards their own country on the Victoria River.[7]

The Killers

The police soon found Jimmy camping close to Bradshaw's Victoria River Station, and he was arrested on 15 August, just over a month after the mutiny. He at first claimed innocence, and that Ivan Egeroff was the murderer. He told Stott "No more, Ivan been killem Georgie. By and bye Jack been say 'No good' killem. By and bye Ivan then been killem Jack."

M.C. Stott then chained Jimmy to a tree near the station homestead and went in search of George. He would later write his report for the Police Court:

> On the 26th August, when the prisoner Jimmy was tied up at Bradshaw's station, he voluntarily stated "George been killem Ivan and Jack, no more me." I took the boy, George [Georgie], in charge at same time and place that I arrested the prisoner Jimmy, but on account of his youth I did not tell him the charge until this morning. He then said that George had pushed Ivan into the water; that Jimmy had cut the rope holding the dingey, and had then caught and held Larson by the neck whilst George shot him in the forehead; that Larson thereupon fell down, and that Jimmy took a tomahawk and struck him on the neck; that George and Jimmy then threw Larson's body overboard, and next washed the blood from the deck; that Jimmy then threw a shot gun, rifle, and revolver into the water. The rifle and revolver produced were handed to me by the prisoner George. When I secured him, he at my request went into the range and brought them to me. There were two cartridges in the revolver, which had not been fired.
>
> ... On the 22nd August I was camped at a spot about 60 miles north-east of Mr. Bradshaw's station, in the ranges. Mr. Palmer, Mr. Bradshaw's head stock man, and Dandy, Larrabi, and a lubra named Judy were with me. There were also five Victoria River natives whose names I do not know. About 1 p.m. I sent these five natives and the two station boys into the ranges to try and induce George to come to my camp, pretending that I was Mr. Bradshaw, and that I wanted to build a camp. They returned about sundown with news that they had seen George with other natives, but that they

were not allowed to get nearer to them than 50 or 60 yards. George told them they were only "gammoning" and that all they wanted was to catch him and tie him up along Mr. Bradshaw's station, all the same Jimmy, and that if they did not immediately go back, he and the natives with him would spear them.

George then took up a spear and threw it at them, saying, "Suppose you strong fellow you come and catchem me now. I no frightened. Suppose anyone come alonga me I kill em." The other natives who were with George then took up their spears, and the station boys, having no firearms, retreated.

On the 23rd August, in company with Mr. Palmer, the station boys, and the five other aborigines, I followed up the tracks of George's mob. After proceeding four miles we came on an abandoned camp. From there we followed fresh tracks about a quarter of a mile further down. All at once I saw about 50 or 60 aboriginals all armed with spears, coming towards us.

I galloped on to them and called out to my party. Dandy said "There's George!" and went after a single native. We galloped through the natives, who threw spears, and all followed Dandy and the native he was after. After going about three quarters of a mile, we abandoned our horses owing to the roughness of the country and continued the chase on foot. We came to a precipice, and Dandy and the native he was pursuing stopped suddenly. Myself and Mr. Palmer were then about thirty yards distant from Dandy. Dandy called out "Come on, Mr. Stott, I got him."

I then called out to the native "You stop, George, in the Queen's name. No more runaway." The native then got hold of one of the jagged spears which he was carrying, and tried to spear Dandy, but owing to the rocky and precipitous character of the foothold he could not throw it with any effect.

When I was about ten yards distant, George disappeared from view down the face, of the cliff. Dandy then fired and struck George in the thick part of the arm. George thereupon slid down the cliff about 40 feet and was again making off when Dandy fired a second shot. The bullet struck George below the shoulder blade on the right side, and he pitched forward quite dead, but still clutching the four spears which he had carried throughout his flight. I may say that it was quite impossible for the party to have followed him any further, and if he had not been shot, he would inevitably have escaped.

The body was afterwards identified by Mr. Palmer, and by Dandy, Larrabi, Judy, and the five natives, as being the identical George who was wanted under a warrant for the murder of John Larson. I afterwards made the natives carry the body to where I was camped, and in my presence, they buried it. Before he was buried, I measured the body of deceased, and found he was six feet high. He was of medium build and had slight scraggy whiskers. I also noticed a slight scum growing over the ball of the right eye. These features tally with the description I received previous to leaving for the Victoria River.[8]

The Police Court

Satisfied that the culprits were either in chains or dead, Stott returned to Port Darwin at the beginning of September 1900[9] and immediately presented Jimmy and young Georgie to Mr. Justice Dashwood in the Police Court. They were dressed as they had been when captured, except for the heavy chains padlocked around their necks, and in the opinion of the *Times*, they "presented an altogether savage and unkempt appearance."[10]

Stott's testimony, of course, was damning, but Ivan Egeroff also needed to appear to answer questions about why Jimmy had accused him. He swore that he had no quarrel with the accused or with Larson that trip and had no reason to kill him, and claimed he had never said "No good, kill 'em", as Jimmy had recounted at first.[11] With a black prisoner in chains, no one suspected him anyway, and there was clearly enough evidence to put Jimmy and Georgie on trial, so they were committed to the Circuit Court later that month.

By then, someone had taken good care to clean them up:

At the examination on Monday last, they again appeared in the dock, but a marvelous metamorphosis had been affected during their brief sojourn out at Fannie Bay. The chains had disappeared, the accumulated dirt of years had been scrubbed from their bodies, and dressed in clean suits of dungaree, they presented such an altered aspect that their own mothers would scarcely have known them.[12]

Up until then, apart from the firearms, it seems few had questioned the whereabouts of the plunder the mutineers had taken from the boat. For instance, there was money in the form of cheques, notes and silver that had never been recovered. The two Daly River men, Cockatoo and Fennem, who were brought to Palmerston as witnesses at the trial said there was a bag of money in their camp, but it was thought that Captain Mugg in the *Minniehaha* would be able to recover it, and other plunder, from the Daly camp when he returned the witnesses to their country.

One item of plunder was more obvious. As Cockatoo stood in the witness box and was asked about the accused, he was, of course, required to wear clothes. How long he was in the witness box goes unrecorded, but it wasn't until he was leaving that Ivan Egeroff recognised the trousers Cockatoo was wearing as his, and he had last seen them on the boat.[13]

It was too late to question him about them while in the dock, and everyone thought it was funny. After consideration however, the editor of the *Times* worried that it seemed:

> … rather too much like turning a terrible tragedy into farce, when witnesses who appear in Court wearing portion of the stolen property are allowed to go Scot free. In fact, is it not rather a mistaken policy to have allowed any of the natives arrested in connection with this affair to return immediately to the neighbourhoods from whence they came. If they had no direct hand in the tragedy itself, there is at least strong presumptive evidence that they have all had more or less to do with the subsequent looting of the vessel, and by permitting their immediate return is it not likely that an impression will be created in the minds of the natives concerned in the affair that the white man does not, after all, view the killing of his countrymen and the plundering of his vessels as a very serious offence.[14]

Chapter 5: Jimmy, 1901

The Circuit Court

The last week of September 1900 was a busy week for Justice Dashwood in the Circuit Court. Other accused murderers were also being tried: Long Peter, "a grizzly and grim-looking old native", was charged with killing another Aboriginal man, coincidentally known as Jimmy, at Pine Creek the previous January. The jury in this case recommended a conviction of manslaughter and Long Peter was sentenced to three months imprisonment with hard labor.

In a break from murder cases, Thomas Hauten pleaded guilty to the assault he was accused of, and was sentenced to three years' imprisonment with hard labor.

Then, in a second murder trial, George Stichling was charged with killing and murdering a Chinese man named Gee Chong Foong, during an argument about the victim's dog, also at Pine Creek. Stichling was given the death sentence, but like many others, it was later commuted.

So, Jimmy and Georgie's trial was just one among several. Justice Dashwood swore in the jurors[15] and an interpreter named Pinchie on the morning of 25 September. The accused were defended by a recent law graduate, the 25-year-old son of Telegraph Superintendent John Little, named Egbert Percy Graham Little.

There was immediate good news. Because Georgie was only about 12 years old, the prosecution announced no plans to produce any evidence against him, so the judge directed the Jury to return a verdict of Not Guilty against him, and he was discharged.

Then the evidence against Jimmy was presented, with testimonies from all the main witnesses heard once again. The trial took most of the day, but at last, late in the afternoon, the judge summed up "at considerable length and with great care… laying special stress upon the value of the testimony furnished by the boy, George." George's testimony impressed him as "being true in every essential particular, and which was corroborated to a great extent by the statements of the other witnesses for the Crown."[16]

But, said the judge:

> ... with regard to the law of the [illegible] they had to consider whether there was sufficient provocation at the time the act was committed to justify them in reducing the charge to manslaughter. In considering the question of the prisoner's guilt, it was not necessary that the evidence should show that his hand had actually dealt the fatal blow. He mentioned this because the counsel for the defence had been to some trouble in endeavouring in cross examination to show that the murdered man, Larson, was dead at the time the prisoner struck the blows with the tomahawk. The fact of Larson being dead at the time those blow were struck would not affect the prisoner's guilt in the slightest degree, if the evidence showed that he was *particeps criminis* – that he had knowledge of what was taking place – and if they were to believe the evidence of the witness George, there could be no doubt that prisoner directly participated in the crime which had taken place.
>
> To reduce the crime to that of manslaughter it must be shown that there was provocation of such a nature as would entitle the prisoner to say "I committed the act on the spur of the moment, in the heat of anger – before my blood had time to cool." He did not think, either as a matter of law or reason, that the facts given in evidence would justify such an assumption. Even granting that the witness Ivan did some time before strike the native George on the back of the neck, he thought it would require more than that to convince the Jury that the prisoner was justified in killing the deceased.
>
> At the same time, it was deeply to be deplored and condemned that people should use ropes or other violent methods in their dealings with these natives. The wilder a native was, the more likely was he to resent such treatment, nurse feelings of revenge, and seize upon the first favorable opportunity for retaliation...[17]

The Verdict

In the evening, the jury retired to consider their verdict. In less than 15 minutes they decided Jimmy was guilty of murder. His Honour then addressed the prisoner and said:

> "Jimmy, you have been found guilty of murder, and upon the evidence there cannot be the slightest doubt that the finding of the Jury is correct. They could come to no other conclusion."

His Honor then passed the solemn death sentence, and the prisoner was removed from the dock.[18]

Jimmy was sent back to his cell to wait the next six months for his sentence to be carried out. His case was, as a matter of course, reviewed by the Executive Committee in Adelaide. If Jimmy was aware of the review he may have held out some hope, but in March the answer came back:

> Our Adelaide correspondent telegraphs that the Cabinet have decided that the death sentence passed on the aboriginal Jimmy for the murder of John Larson, at the mouth of the Daly River, in the Northern Territory, shall be carried into effect. The execution is to take place as near as possible to the scene of the outrage.[19]

Taking the condemned to the scene of the crime, as they had done for Moolooloorun, seemed a good way to send a warning to the tribe. It was approved under the *Criminal Law Consolidation Act* (1876), but it was not particularly useful in this case, because Jimmy's country was near the Victoria River, not the Daly, where he had committed the murder. So, by the beginning of April, the authorities decided to vary the approach and take Jimmy back to his clan's land for his execution. It was announced that "the prisoner will be hanged in his native district as a warning to the tribes."[20]

The Execution

On 2 April 1901, Deputy-Sheriff John Little, several policemen, and a hangman, chained Jimmy to the chartered *Thomas Andrea* and set sail for the Victoria River. Bradshaw's Run was not far from the banks of a tributary known as Shaw's Creek (now called Angalarri River) and after days of motoring they unloaded makeshift gallows and constructed it on the riverbank, while Jimmy's clan gathered around and waited.

It all went well, reported the *Times*, after the *Thomas Andrea* returned ten days later:

> ... No hitch occurred in carrying out the grim object of the expedition. The gallows was erected within a few hundred yards of Bradshaw's station, and the black murderer was duly swung off at the appointed hour in the presence of some 50 of his countrymen. Accounts differ as to the apparent effect of the ghastly and novel spectacle upon the blacks – but it should need to be deep and permanent to justify all this bother and expense.[21]

Endnotes

1. Ivan Egeroff was a violent man who is known to have whipped his Aboriginal workers. He was later killed in the 'Bradshaw Massacre' along with Fred Bradshaw, Ernest Dannock and Jerry Skeahan, in 1905 (see Lewis, 2022).
2. Harry Neimann and his family had recently taken over the Daly River Mission buildings abandoned by the Jesuit missionaries. Neimann was experimenting with producing cattle and buffalo meat extracts, while employing local Aboriginal hunters to bring him the skins of birds, crocodiles, and snakes to on-sell, at the cost of a half a stick of tobacco paid to the hunters.
3. *NTTGG*, 20 July 1900, page 3: Reported Outrage by Blacks on the Daly River. The launch Wunwulla seized by the natives.
4. *NTTGG*, Friday 20 July 1900, page 3: Reported Outrage by Blacks on the Daly River. the launch Wunwulla seized by the natives.
5. Constable Frederick Stuckey Stone served the force from 1888 until 1901.
6. *Daily Telegraph*, 7 August 1900, page 5: The Daly River Outrage: How the Crime was Committed.
7. *Bathurst Free Press and Mining Journal*, 8 August 1900, page 2.
8. *NTTGG*, 7 September 1900, page 3: Daly River Outrage. Arrest of two of the alleged principals at Victoria River, one of the alleged culprits shot.
9. *NTTGG*, 7 September 1900, page 3: Daly River Outrage. Arrest of two of the alleged principals at Victoria River, one of the alleged culprits shot.
10. *NTTGG*, 10 August 1900, page 3: News and Notes.
11. *NTTGG*, 7 September 1900, page 3: Daly River Outrage. Arrest of two of the alleged principals at Victoria River, one of the alleged culprits shot.
12. *NTTGG*, 10 August 1900, page 3: News and Notes.
13. *NTTGG*, 10 August 1900, page 3: News and Notes.
14. *NTTGG*, 10 August 1900, page 3: News and Notes.
15. The Jury was Messrs. Stevenson, Johns, Luxton, Whiteford, McKeddie, Lawrie, Pinder, Wedd, Riddell, McPherson, Witherden, and Captain Mugg. The last is a surprise: given his involvement on the Minniehaha, Captain Mugg was unlikely to have been an impartial juror.
16. *NTTGG*, 28 September 1900, page 3: Circuit Court.
17. *NTTGG*, 28 September 1900, page 3: Circuit Court.
18. *NTTGG*, 28 September 1900, page 3: Circuit Court.
19. *Brisbane Courier*, 7 March 1901, page 4: The Northern Territory Murder.
20. *Evening Star*, Thursday 4 April 1901, page 4: Victoria River Murder.
21. *NTTGG*, 12 April 1901, page 3.

Hanged: Execution in the Top End

Chapter 6
Alligator River Tommy, 1905

Hanged in Fannie Bay Gaol on 21 December 1905, for the murders of Henry Edwards, Richard Frost and Nowra.[1]

'Alligator River' Tommy was a cattleman happy to travel across the Territory for work. He was born among the tribes of the Alligator Rivers, east of Palmerston, but committed his crimes on Victoria River Downs Station, some thousand kilometres to the southwest. Tommy was described as a "fine specimen of a native, of exceptional intelligence, over six feet in height and of athletic build, with an open and frank face and demeanour and erect carriage."[2]

The events that ended his life occurred on 11 January 1905, near an outstation on Victoria River Downs Station called Longreach.

The Victims

Henry Edwards, Richard "Dick" Frost, and Henry "Dutchy" Benning were yard-building for the station. On that day Frost was ill and had stayed in the camp with a pregnant Aboriginal woman named Nowra (aka Nora).

Edwards and Benning were carting timber into camp when they heard several gunshots. Assuming Frost was shooting turkeys, they thought nothing of it, until a shot rang out from nearby, and dirt was knocked up in the road before them. It was an ambush.

Benning, who was on horseback driving the team, said he

saw smoke rising from behind green bushes twenty yards away and Tommy step from behind the bushes with a rifle in his hand. He shouted to Edwards, "For Christ's sake, get off the dray; there's that black bastard Tommy trying to shoot you!"[3]

Edwards' final words were: "What are you doing, boy?"

Tommy ran round the back of the dray and fired at Edwards, who sank backwards. He then fired two shots at Benning, who spurred his horse and galloped back to Longreach, followed part of the way by Tommy, who fired at least four or five more times.

Benning returned the next morning with Tom Cusack, another station contractor, and recalled that:

> ... the horses had moved only a short distance and were still harnessed. Edwards was found lying face downwards on his folded arms, dead. A bullet had entered one side below the ribs and had made its exit on the other side.[4]

Benning and Cusack then went to the camp to find Frost:

> ... He was lying down, with bullet wound, which had entered left side of head, come out below the left eye, re-entered the left shoulder, and remained embedded in muscle of the left arm. He was lying on a bag with a pillow under his head. Bone and brain matter were protruding from the wound. He was alive but unconscious. Found the lubra Nora in a gully running into the creek, about 90 yards from camp. She was dead. She had a bullet wound in the breast, high up. She was lying face downwards, her face resting on her crossed arms and crouching on her knees.[5]

Frost died the next day without ever regaining consciousness.

The Killer

It took nearly a month to track Tommy down and arrest him. Mounted Constable James Kelly, helped by Cecil Freer, found him at the Great Western Mine[6] on 12 February. Freer knew Tommy well as he had employed him several times as a buffalo shooter and claimed that he was "one of the best shots among the natives so employed."[7]

During the pre-trial in July before Justice Herbert,[8] Freer's

Chapter 6: Alligator River Tommy, 1905

testimony included a written record of a lengthy conversation the two had, after Freer had handcuffed Tommy to a tree:

… I asked him if he knew that I was looking for him. He said "Yes."

I said, "What did you want to run away from me for?"

He said, "Because I was frightened."

I asked him what he had to be frightened about. He said, "Because I done something."

I then asked him where he had been, and he replied, "Out Victoria River way with Edwards."

I asked him if there was anybody else out there with them, and he said, "Yes, Dick and Dutchy."

I asked if Campbell's half-caste children were out there. He said "Yes, they are out there." I said, "What are they?" he said, "A girl and a boy." I said, "Which one did you shoot?"

He said, "O no, not that one; black lubra."

I said, "What did you shoot Edwards for?"

He said, "Because he is too cheeky."

I said, "Why did you shoot Frost?"

He said, "All the same."

I said, "What do you mean by cheeky?"

He said, "Oh, he hit me and swear at me."

I said, "Who hit you?"

He said, "Edwards."

I said, "When did he hit you?"

He said, "On the road out to Victoria."

I said, "What did he hit you for?"

He said, "O, can't find 'em horses sometimes quick."

I said, "What did he hit you with?"

He said, "One time with mosquito net peg; another time with stock whip."

He said, "One time when they growl and hit me with a stick, I hear Dick say to Edwards "Better give the bugger a bullet; he is too lazy; and put him in a hole." Three days after that I shot 'em."

I said, "Who did you shoot first?"

He said, "Dick."⁹

This conversation was later judged to be inadmissible in the trial by Justice Herbert, but by the time the legal arguments were all heard, the jury was certainly aware of it.

The Trial

Alligator River Tommy's trial took several days. In the end, after reading the whole of the evidence aloud, Herbert asked the jury to retire and make their decision. It did not take long. When they returned, they announced that they had found the prisoner guilty.

There was then a display of emotion, one journalist noted, but not from the prisoner:

> His Honor then formally sentenced the prisoner to death, and as he concluded uttering the dread and solemn phrases, he exhibited signs of considerable emotion. More so than the prisoner, who received the sentence with outward apathy.[10]

Alligator River Tommy then had four months within which to lodge an appeal.

Tommy may have taken the news calmly, but he was not a man to sit around and wait when opportunities arise. After just a few days in the gaol, Palmerston was "thrown into a state of excitement by the startling news, telephoned in from Fannie Bay Gaol, to the effect that the condemned murderer, Tommy, had succeeded in breaking bounds and effecting his escape."[11]

The warden, Mr A. G. Strath and his wife, lived in a house next to the gaol. There was a connecting gateway, which was usually locked, but:

> Tommy had just been allowed outside his cell for a smoke, as was customary. At the moment Guard Sprigg's attention was called elsewhere by one of the other prisoners, and he temporarily abandoned his supervision of Tommy. He was absent but a short time, and on returning found Tommy had disappeared, and at the same time heard screams from

Mrs. Strath, who was alone in the house, and who explained that she had heard the clanking of the prisoner's chains as he bounded through the gaoler's private residence… The gateway dividing the gaol yard from Mr. Strath's private quarters would appear to have been left open, and there seems to be no doubt that prisoner had keenly noted this, and taking advantage of the warder's temporary absence elsewhere, he seized the opportunity to make a dash for freedom.[12]

Tommy had managed to slip through the open gate but the chase was on as soon as Mrs Strath's screams raised the alarm. Tommy fled into the forest, still wearing his leg-irons, followed soon after by Mounted Constables Johnston and Kelly, and several trackers. They found Tommy's tracks but lost them somewhere near Armstrong's Farm (now Nightcliff), believing that Tommy's countrymen aided the escapee by physically carrying him through the bush.

Tommy was free for just two days, but his recapture raised questions. He was:

> … recaptured in the yard of the Palmerston Police Station at about 20 minutes past 9 p.m. on Wednesday evening, by George Wedd, who, curiously enough, was one of the Jury empaneled to try the prisoner at his recent trial and condemnation.[13]

Wedd recognised Tommy as he walked into M.C. Kelly's yard, and he grabbed him by the wrists. Tommy made no effort at resistance, and when locked in a cell at the police station, a crowd soon gathered to view him:

> … He appeared tired but quite cool and unconcerned. In reply to a query as to why he had been such a fool to come back, his eyes gleamed for a moment half savagely, and he then replied, with a smile "O, no matter!" He had got rid of the chain, but the irons were still on both ankles. In reply to queries he said the chain had been cut off with a tomahawk. He had also shaved off the small tuft of beard worn during his trial. He was given a blanket. He then asked for some cigarettes (a wooden pipe had a few minutes previously been taken away from him), and to all outward appearance was prepared to accept the situation with cheerful stoicism.[14]

Tommy later claimed he had returned to give himself up, but it was also guessed that he was trying to find weapons that he could steal and begin more active resistance. After all, said the *Times*, "the prisoner is a native of quite exceptional intelligence" and he had "brains enough to plan such a scheme."[15]

But Tommy was returned to his cell to await his fate and never given another chance to escape. His four-month appeal time finished on 5 November, but it took almost two more months for the hanging to be arranged. The delay was inexcusable, said the *Times*, for the mental anguish that Tommy must have suffered:

> Such negligence is not only scandalous but cruel. Although we do not suppose that Tommy – who according to last reports, was sleek and happy – is eating his heart out in anxious suspense, still such procrastination is unexcusable [sic]. Imagine the condition of an intelligent white prisoner similarly placed.[16]

The Execution

Tommy was hanged at Fannie Bay Gaol at 9 a.m. on Thursday morning, 21 December 1905:

> … When first brought from his cell Tommy displayed some slight symptoms of agitation but speedily regained his usual stoical calmness during the reading of the formal warrant. He made no statement and marched on to the scaffold with a firm step and coolly adjusted his feet whilst his legs were being pinioned. The cap was then drawn over his head, the signal given, the bolt instantly drawn, and Tommy was launched into eternity. The grim drama occupied only a few minutes, and was carried through without a single hitch, death being apparently almost instantaneous.[17]

When Tommy was waiting on death row, he shared his cell with a murderer named Benamulla who, instead of the gallows, had been given a three-year sentence for killing the abuser of his wife.

Perhaps it was a reasonable penalty, but there was possibly more to Benamulla's story than what the court heard. As Alligator River

Chapter 6: Alligator River Tommy, 1905

Figure 13: Fannie Bay Gaol (undated, LANT, ph0002-0085, Roger Nott Collection).

Tommy was climbing the scaffold, he was accompanied by Reverend D. Fletcher, and the chaplain later recalled an odd comment made by Tommy, almost as the noose was being placed around his neck:

> "Benamulla plenty gammon – tell plenty lies – get three years. Me talk all about true – me hang!"[18]

Endnotes

1. Much of this chapter comes from my book Darwin: End of an Era (Pugh 2025).
2. *NTTGG*, 22 December 1905, page 3.
3. *NTTGG*, 10 March 1905, page 2.
4. *Advertiser*, 7 March 1905, page 4.
5. *NTTGG*, 10 March 1905, page 2.
6. The Great Western Mine was near the Margaret River diggings, about 100 km south of Darwin.
7. *NTTGG*, 10 March 1905, page 2.
8. Justice Herbert succeeded Charles Dashwood on February 1, 1905.
9. *NTTGG*, 10 March 1905, page 2.
10. *NTTGG*, 7 July 1905, page 3.
11. *NTTGG*, 14 July 1905, page 2.
12. *NTTGG*, 14 July 1905, page 2.
13. *NTTGG*, 14 July 1905, page 3.
14. *NTTGG*, 14 July 1905, page 3.
15. *NTTGG*, 14 July 1905, page 3.
16. *NTTGG*, 1 December 1905, page 2.
17. *NTTGG*, 22 December 1905, page 3.
18. *NTTGG*, 22 December 1905, page 3.

Chapter 7
Koppio, 1913

Hanged in Fannie Bay Gaol on 15 July 1915, for the murders of Ching Loy and Lo Sin near the Old Howley Mine.

The Victims

North of Pine Creek the modern Stuart Highway cuts directly through the goldfields that have been the basis of mining in the area since nuggets were first found in telegraph pole holes by linesmen in 1871. By 1874 a gold rush was in full flow, and thousands of miners, the majority of them Chinese men, turned up to wash the soil and extract the precious metal. Several small settlements grew to support them, and batteries were installed to crush the ore.

The first village was Yam Creek - where Chee Hang was murdered by Chung Yeung and Lem Kai in 1899. Yam Creek was followed by Brocks Creek, Burrundie, and mining camps that sprung up at every and any likely location. One of them was on Howley Creek, named after an Overland Telegraph Line worker. 'The Howley,' as it was known, supported many alluvial mining companies to various levels of success. It still does. Modern travelers these days who pass the Howley Mine area at 130 kilometres per hour along the Stuart Highway remain unaware of the huge modern Cosmo-Howley Mine that now produces gold from deeper in the same ground, a few hundred metres to their west.

In 1912, however, the Howley stampers were silent and most of the surface gold had long gone. Nevertheless, a few people were still scratching a living there, and two of them were Chinese miners named Lo Sin and Ching Loy. They were well past the age of 60, and they lived in two small huts, surrounded by a garden of sweet potatoes, peanuts, custard apple trees, mangoes, and bananas. The garden was so productive that the two were almost self-sufficient, and rarely did they venture away from the area.

Sometime during November that year, the elderly men were visited by other men ready to murder them for their food and equipment. Their black and swollen bodies were discovered by a Chinese fruit and vegetable hawker named Ah Lin a few days later, each with a spear wound in their back. The men were old friends who Ah Lin had not seen for some time but:

> … on getting near he could see no sign of life, and then his eyes fell on a gruesome object in the shape of a blackened and putrid human hand protruding from beneath some sheets of old galvanized iron.[1]

Ah Lin did not stop to make further investigations but hurried at once to Mounted Constable John (Jack) Johns at Brocks Creek Police Station,[2] and Johns and his trackers, Larry, Paddy 'Disher' Bradshaw, and Tommy, rode out and investigated the murder.[3] By the time they arrived, the men had then been dead for about a week. Johns spared no details in his report to the court:

> … Bodies covered with three sheets of corrugated iron… lying within about 6 feet of Loy's house and practically touching one another; one was of a big Chinaman, other of a small one. Body of big man on broad of back, arms outstretched, clothed in dungaree trousers and small belt; left hand and part of forearm were missing; right hand minus 1st and 2nd joints of index and 2nd fingers; these had a chewed off appearance; small starved dog present; wound, clean cut, about two inches in length under left shoulder blade of the body, whilst a smaller wound was visible under right breast, appearing as if weapon used in thrust had protruded there from back.

Chapter 7: Koppio, 1913

Figure 14: M.C. John (Jack) Johns with Trackers (L-R) Delta, Yurunditba, and Koolmutchki. Johns employed a Chinese tailor in Pine Creek to make unofficial uniforms for his team (1911, SLSA, B-20201).

Body of smaller man lying face downward, slightly inclined on left shoulder; wound about 4 inches below nape of neck on this body, similar to wound under left shoulder blade of other body. No sign of any struggle. Rain had fallen prior to my arrival and no tracks visible.⁴

Johns collected a coroner's warrant to bury the bodies, and he and his trackers had the unpleasant duty of digging a grave for them outside their shack, while a Chinese priest set off several hundred firecrackers to drive away the evil spirits.

The motive for the murders was immediately apparent – the old men's huts had been ransacked, and food, blankets and clothing had gone. Johns, who had only just returned from a patrol, knew that a further trip would be necessary to track down the killers, so he returned to Brocks Creek to prepare.

He was ready with his trackers on 1 December with a plant of 16 horses and the equipment needed for an extended patrol. They camped the first night at Douglas Hot Springs and then went overland to the Daly River. Johns interviewed every Aboriginal person he met, and listening to the gossip, it was not long before he had the names of three suspects: Koppio, Katterinyan, and Anyuana. Johns already knew Koppio, but the other two were strangers to him, although the three had passed by Daly River some weeks before, with two women, a boy, and an old man. "Koppio was a partly civilized black" wrote Johns "belonging to the Fitzmaurice River country, one of the least known parts of the Northern Territory. Katterinyan and Anyuana were practically uncivilized."⁵

Following them to the river, and crossing it at a safe place upstream, Johns later realised he was on the wrong side when he saw campfire smoke rising from the forest on the opposite bank. Suspecting that his quarry might still be in the area, he ignored potential crocodile attacks and recrossed the river at once and silently approached a group of people resting around the fires. He sent the trackers around the camp to prevent anyone from escaping and when they were in position, Johns rushed in with his revolvers drawn.

The people in the camp were surprised, but as most were Daly River residents familiar with Johns, they did not react strongly. Among them was Koppio. According to Johns, his sudden arrival resulted in

Chapter 7: Koppio, 1913

Koppio being "bailed up" without resistance and a neck-chain was locked around his neck. He was subsequently led everywhere on foot by a mounted tracker.

The young man impressed Johns:

> Koppio was a splendid specimen of a black. He stood over six feet three inches in height, was about 12 stone in weight, and I should say he was about 25 years of age. For rewards of tobacco and clothing he would carry two 70 lb. bags of flour on his head from the Chinese store at Daly River, lower downstream to the fossickers, both white and Chinese, as far away as forty miles. By this class of work, he was in exceptionally good trim.[6]

Unfortunately, Katterinyan and Anyuana had already left the Daly River to return to the Fitzmaurice River region, 250 kilometres away. It would be a grueling long patrol, especially for Koppio, chained and on foot, but Johns was committed to following them. Within a week he had come across the old man, Napoo[7], and the 10-year-old boy who had been present at the time of the murder. They had been left behind by Katterinyan and Anyuana, as Napoo had a "bad foot" and could not travel as quickly.

Several days and many miles later, the plant arrived at the Fitzmaurice River. They located an Aboriginal camp at the base of an escarpment without being seen. The only occupants were old men, women, and children, so they quietly left them and returned later to hide in the long grass until the young men cam back with the products of their days' foraging.

> In the gathering twilight my trackers crawled to the foot of the cliff beside the camp, and I walked straight at the camp. I was within 30 yards of the camp when a young man spotted me. He gave a startled cry. Neither trackers or myself had seen Katterinyan or Anyuana before, but two young blacks darted up and away for the cliff, and in doing so ran right into the guns of my trackers. They turned out to be the two I was after.[8]

The two new prisoners were handcuffed and chained together

Figure 15: Aboriginal prisoners were chained together and forced to walk to Darwin to face the courts. In this photo by Francis Birtles, four alleged killers of 'Brigalow Bill' Ward were brought in by MC Holland in 1910 (Birtles Collection, ex Lewis, 2022).

with the heavy neck chains they would have to carry on the long trek back to Brocks Creek. Their wives were also held as witnesses.

Johns was very pleased with himself as he and his party started the long journey overland, but his three prisoners and the witnesses were on foot, so the progress was slow. They were still in the bush on Christmas Day, and they celebrated by eating a brolga Johns had shot, plus the final tin of salmon from his original rations. After that, it was another eight days before he was home, and the party had to live off the land.

Johns must have reflected on the efforts of his patrol as they trudged through the wilderness back to Brocks Creek. The journey had tested every ounce of endurance, with days blending into nights through unforgiving terrain. The prisoners, bound in chains, were resigned to their fate, but Johns needed to remain vigilant, knowing full well that his task was far from complete.

At last, in Brocks Creek, the three prisoners attended a 'summary hearing' before a local justice of the peace, and a day or two later were on the train to Darwin, committed to trial for murder at the Supreme Court.

As he recounted the events to the inspector upon his return, Johns' achievements seemed monumental.

Exhausted, Johns returned home to Brocks Creek for a rest – but not for long.

Escape

Word was sent a few days later that the three accused had escaped.[9] Johns was horrified, but he returned to duty. With his horses knocked up from the previous patrol, he chose an alternative method to travel. He chartered a railway push trolley, much to the delight of Larry, Paddy Disher and Tommy, and they again set out to capture the fugitives.

They only went as far as Darwin River. There was only one track south out of Darwin, and they waited in ambush beside the river crossing for a couple of days. With no sign of the escapees, they returned south to stake out the Adelaide River railway bridge. Relying on his growing formidable reputation, Johns asked the local Aboriginal clan, who were camped nearby, for help.

> All went well until about 3 a.m. the same night, when, to my delight I saw the black form of a lubra crawling towards me and the trackers… She had been sent to tell me that Koppio, tired and hungry, had just arrived at the camp and that he had told them that he had left Katterinyan and Anyuana the first day out from gaol, and had not seen them since. He thought they had been rearrested. My trackers were all excitement. The gin indicated the spot where Koppio lay. We surrounded the spot and had an easy win. He was grabbed and that was really the end of the career of Koppio.[10]

But the other two had gotten clean away. There was nothing for it but for Johns and his trackers to return to the Fitzmaurice River area to recapture them. But there was no hurry – Johns needed to be sure his horses were fit and ready to go first, and that was just as well because the patrol lasted three months. It was the longest patrol Johns would ever do. Several horses were lost on the way, including one to a crocodile when crossing a river, but he caught both Katterinyan and Anyuana, plus a thief named Corrigan, and returned them all to gaol. Their journey was extended because, out of rations, they needed to detour to the Chinese store on the bank of the Victoria River.

Anyuana, back in court, pleaded guilty to the charge of escaping from prison. He was sentenced to six months imprisonment and, for his involvement in the murder, a *nolle prosequi* was entered and no further proceedings were taken against him.[11] He was later called as a witness against Katterinyan.

Because it took so long to capture them, Koppio had been tried while the others were still on the run. That meant, in the end, he was to die alone.

Koppio's Trial

Mounted Constable Johns was not present at Koppio's trial because he was on patrol looking for Koppio's co-accused, but he had done a remarkable job in collecting and organising the evidence:

> … the feature of the trial was the careful and elaborate marshalling of all the facts and exhibits connected with the case for the Crown by the police officer entrusted with the charge of the case - M.C. Johns.

Several witnesses were examined:

> … of whom a small boy and a lubra showed remarkable natural intelligence. The lubra, in describing some of the scenes in the tragedy of which she had been eyewitness, displayed an aptitude for dramatically expressive action which would have done no discredit to a trained histrionic.

The case lasted the whole day, and the jury found Koppio guilty:

> His Honor formally passed the dread death sentence upon Koppio, who betrayed no emotion, presumably, because he did not understand.[12]

Chapter 7: Koppio, 1913

Figure 16: Judge J D J Bevan (undated, LANT, ph0412-0174).

Debate about the location for the hanging.

A memorandum to Prime Minister Cook from Minister for External Affairs Patrick Glynn in June 1913 explained the crime, the trial and the verdict.[13] Glynn recommended that Koppio's death penalty be carried out. There was, he noted, no recommendation for mercy from the jury, and there were "no facts to justify the prerogative of mercy."

The judge consulted Chief Protector of Aborigines William Stretton and the superintendent of Alligator River Reserve, Paddy Cahill, about the process, because of their long experience in the Territory. At the time, Cahill was also a Protector of Aboriginals, and an inspector under the Aboriginal ordinance. To be thorough, Bevan also sought the opinion of Professor Baldwin Spencer (through Government Secretary Henry Carey) because he was about to take over from Stretton as Chief Protector just a few months later.

Paddy Cahill, whose reputation as a buffalo hunter and skilled horseman preceded him, felt that if the execution took place on country, the body should be cremated and Stretton agreed. This would be, said Stretton, "the greatest deterrent."[14] However, if the execution took place in the gaol, it would only work as a deterrent if "middle-aged members" of his tribe were present as witnesses.

Professor Spencer was also "very insistent" that the best possible deterrent effect of the execution would be to hang Koppio in his native country, in front of his countrymen.[15]

So, Justice Bevan telegraphed Minister Glynn:
BEGINS I CONSIDER THAT EXECUTION AT DARWIN WOULD BE NO MORE A DETERRENT THAN IMPRISONMENT FOR LIFE AT DARWIN. WOULD RECOMMEND THAT THE DEATH SENTENCE BE COMMUTED. IF, HOWEVER, SENTENCE OF DEATH BE EXECUTED IN THE COUNTRY OF THE CONDEMNED PRISONER THIS WOULD HAVE AN UNDOUBTED GREAT DETERRENT EFFECT AND I WOULD NOT, IN THIS CASE RECOMMEND COMMUTATION. THERE IS NOTHING IN THE EVIDENCE ITSELF TO FORM GROUND FOR RECOMMENDING THE SENTENCE BE COMMUTED ENDS SUGGEST DISCUSSION WITH ADMINISTRATOR BEFORE ACTION TAKEN[16]

Was Bevan suggesting that the execution take place on country because it would be a greater deterrent to other Aboriginals to avoid murdering Chinese people? Administrator Gilruth certainly thought so:

EXECUTION IN NATIVE COUNTRY DESIRABLE STOP PAST EXPERIENCE OF SUCH EXECUTIONS HAS PROVED MOST EFFICACIOUS STOP[17]

But by April 1913, the judge needed to be pushed to make up

his mind. Attorney General W. M. Hughes had read all the telegrams and letters and complained that none of them were clear as to what the judge wanted. Therefore, it was:

> Desirable that the judge should be asked to state formerly and fully in writing exactly what course he recommends.[18]

Hughes was against the idea of cremation:

> The Government ought not in any circumstances agree… To dispose of the body in a manner quite unusual with us and unknown to the aboriginals might very well be regarded by them as a desecration and would certainly shock the feelings of a large section of the white community…[19]

The archives hold no other comments of Justice Bevan's deliberations. However, by 3 July the decision was made. Minister Glynn wrote:

> … Cabinet has considered the matter and has decided that the law shall take its course. Arrangements should be made for the necessary recommendation to the Governor General in Council. Execution to be in Darwin Gaol.[20]

So, unlike the previous executions of Aboriginal murderers, Koppio was *not* taken to his home country to be hanged in front of his clan. Minister Glynn told the Administrator that Cabinet had given no "expression of opinion as to the presence of natives at the execution other than to decide that no compulsion is to be exercised to secure their attendance."[21]

So that was that. The execution was given the go ahead.

The Execution

The newspapers told the public that Koppio was to be executed on 18 July 1913. But three days before that, he was given his final meal, led from his cell, and quietly taken to the prison gallows. It was a simple ruse – the government was aware that executions in the southern cities drew large crowds, and this might have led to trouble.[22]

Koppio climbed the steps of the gallows with his arms pinioned. A white hood was placed over his head, and then the noose. The lever was pulled, the trap dropped, and Koppio was "hanged by his neck until his body was dead."[23]

So, in the end, there were no volunteer "middle-aged compatriots" around to witness his death, although presumably other prisoners had already dug his grave in the prison cemetery. Perhaps they were on stand-by to fill it in.

Eight white men witnessed the execution: the acting sheriff, the gaoler, three guards, the medical officer, a priest, and the unnamed hangman.

Koppio had probably never felt so alone, but he appears to have gone to his death calmly and quietly. Shame then, on the *Townsville Daily Bulletin*, who seemed to revel in the tragedy, and were happy to make things up:

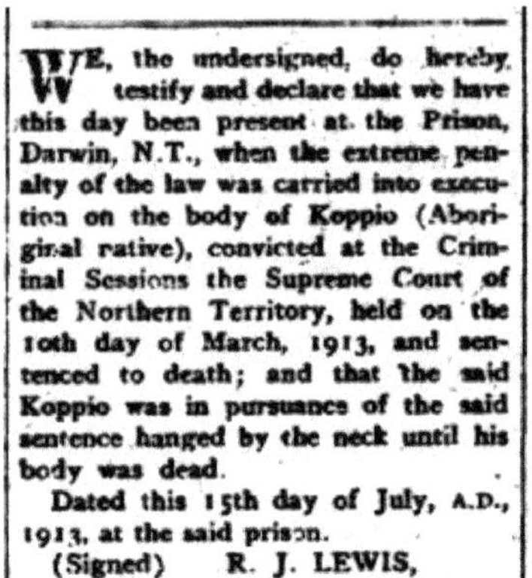

WE, the undersigned, do hereby testify and declare that we have this day been present at the Prison, Darwin, N.T., when the extreme penalty of the law was carried into execution on the body of Koppio (Aboriginal native), convicted at the Criminal Sessions the Supreme Court of the Northern Territory, held on the 10th day of March, 1913, and sentenced to death; and that the said Koppio was in pursuance of the said sentence hanged by the neck until his body was dead.

Dated this 15th day of July, A.D., 1913, at the said prison.

(Signed) R. J. LEWIS, Actg. Sheriff.
A. G. STRATH, Gaoler.
G. P. GOODMAN, Guard.
A. R. LEWIS, Guard.
R. WOOD, Temporary Guard.

I CECIL L. STRANGMAN, being the Medical Officer in attendance on the execution of Koppio at the Prison at Darwin, N.T., do hereby certify and declare that the said Koppio was, in pursuance of the sentence of the Court, hanged by the neck until his body was dead.

Given under my hand this 15th day of July, in the year of our Lord One thousand nine hundred and thirteen, at the said Prison.

(Sgd.) CECIL L. STRANGMAN, Medical Officer.

Figure 17: Office of the Administrator's announcement confirming Koppio's execution, (*NTTGG*, 17 July 1913).

> The execution of Koppio, an aborigine, who was concerned in the murder of two Chinamen at Howley, was carried out at Fannie Bay Prison today. Koppio, in contra-distinction to the customary impassivity of the aborigine when about to die, was completely unnerved, and fought desperately for life. His screams could be heard for a wide radius round the gaol, and several natives who were passing ran terror stricken from the vicinity. Anyuana, a countryman, who was implicated to a lesser extent in the murder, when led to see the corpse lying in the coffin, trembled violently and fell ill.[24]

Mounted Constable Johns, who had worked so hard to catch

Chapter 7: Koppio, 1913

Koppio and his colleagues, was not present. However, he was not forgotten because Judge Bevan rewarded him with fifteen pounds for his "conspicuous service in sheeting home a charge of murder."[25]

Katterinyan's Trial

Koppio's partner in the crime, Katterinyan, was tried on 14 July 1913, four months after Koppio was condemned and coincidentally, on the day before Koppio was hanged.

Justice Bevan and the jury had a lot to listen to in Katterinyan's trial. Mounted Constable Johns had collected about a dozen witnesses who could testify and had massed a huge amount of evidence against the accused – including parts of a red blanket and Chinese clothing found both in the victims' houses and in the camps. The evidence and the witnesses, of course, had previously been used in Koppio's trial, so there must have been an expectation that the verdict would be the same. As it turned out, it was not, but the following information is included here became records of the equivalent proceedings of Koppio's trial have been lost.

Anyuana was the first to stand in the dock at both Koppio's and Katterinyan's trials. In the latter, a translator named McGill translated his statement into English:

> Me been camp along old fellow's house; I savvy old chinamen… Been camp with Katterinyan, Koppio, Napoo, my little brother, Womberia and Kolbung; morning time chinamen been talk "you go away, by and by policemen come." We all about go away; Katterinyan, Koppio and I been hunt kangaroo; Koppio been kill em kangaroo; by and by been come back and eat em up; Katterinyan and Koppio been catchem silver, take him along Ah Man's store; another one Chinaman been give it silver, been buy flour along Ah Man's store, been bringem flour and bake em Johnnycake and eat em. Old man been sit down behind; other six been go away; go along garden, two fellow man been sit down along garden, two fellow Chinaman. One been work garden, been use shovel, cleaning grass; big fellow Ah Loy, other one been sit

89

down along house. Koppio been fetch em up spear and plant him along garden; only two spears.

Black fellow been go along big fellow Chinaman; Koppio been ask em matches; Chinamen been talk "you go away, I can't give it," Koppio no been stand up long way, been stand close up; Ah Loy been talk "you go away." Chinaman try hit him with shovel and Ah Loy wrestle; Ah Loy hurt em finger. Chinaman go along house; Koppio been run and catchem spear; Koppio been talk "we been kill em, might shoot em' Koppio been give one fellow spear to Katterinyan and been have himself too. Katterinyan took em up spear, chuck him and kill em along here (showing back), just come out here, pointing to his chest. Koppio been take em spear too and kill em little Chinaman, (pointing to his back) no more come out. Ah Loy been lose em gun. Little fellow Chinaman fall down, big fellow stagger. Big fellow take out other fellow Chinaman's spear first time, by em bye pull em out spear himself and fall down. Two fellow Chinaman dead. Kolbung, Womberia, Mattacaeyah and I went frightened; been race. Go sit along hill.[26]

In Anyuana's version of the story, Koppio and Katterinyan gathered everybody back again, and together they raided the huts, taking a mosquito net, trousers, flour and rice, a tomahawk, and a knife, plus squares of the red blanket and other things labelled and tendered as evidence. On cross examination, Anyuana said that Koppio had told him "I been catchem spear, Chinaman might shoot me," suggesting some element of self-defense, but he had not seen the gun himself.

When Kolbung was called as a witness, she said that the three accused had discussed killing the old men:

... three fellow blackfellow talk "More better kill em, can't catch em policemen." Koppio and Katterinyan have em spear, hook em up along woomera; Katterinyan first time. I been see em. Katterinyan been throw first, Koppio behind.[27]

In cross-examination Kolbung said she had seen Katterinyan and "little fellow" wrestle. She said that Katterinyan, not Koppio, had been hit with the shovel, and Ah Loy ran to get his gun. She then saw Ah Loy put his gun to his shoulder and point it at Katterinyan, who ducked, but he then threw the spear.

Womberia's testimony was objected to by the defence:

> An objection by Mr. Roberts to admitting the evidence of one of the female witnesses, on the ground that she was the wife of one of the accused, was overruled by His Honor, who argued that marriage as between aboriginal natives could not be regarded as a legal ceremony under English law.[28]

Her version was similar anyway, except that she thought that Koppio collected the spears only after he feared Ah Loy was fetching his gun:

> Ah Loy been catch em gun; Chinaman catch em gun first time, blackfellow catch em spear behind. Chinaman come out from door, look round no more boy outside. Katterinyan hook up spear along woomera, chuck em and kill em Ah Loy.[29]

The other woman present, Mattacajaiah, who called Nappoo the "old man," said that Koppio had been wrestling with Ah Loy, but agreed that Katterinyan was the one hit with a shovel. There was, as would be expected, a little confusion about the events, but all agreed that Katterinyan's spear had killed Ah Loy, and Koppio's spear had killed Lo Sin.

Crown Prosecutor Ross Mallam then called the police trackers who had accompanied Mounted Constable Johns to the murder scene and seen the bodies, and then rested his case.

Katterinyan's defence was given quickly by Counsellor Donald Roberts[30] and Katterinyan made a statement, supported by an interpreter named Possum:

> I savee sit down along Chinaman's house. Two men go look out for kangaroo, Koppio and Katterinyan; catch em all right; come back catch em two lubra and little boy and old man. Womberia my lubra. I bin let lubra go along Chinaman's house. Chinaman bin give em two fellow money; lubra say I get two fellow money, you take em. I bin big fellow growl along lubra. I bin go along Chinaman's store buy em flour. Come back along camp, bake em johnnycakes. Bake em and cook em and eat em, all about bin eat em. Camped there all night, another night go along another Chinaman, go along

Chinaman's house and get em bread, bin eat em. Bin go another one's house, been go along Ah Sin's house. Koppio been go first time, I bin go behind. Koppio been go straight up Ah Loy's house and ask for matches; I bin come up behind, bin stand up a little bit long way, Koppio bin close up Ah Loy. I bin stand up along one place.

Koppio bin ask Ah Loy matches. Ah Loy say "go away." Koppio no more go away, stand up. Ah Loy hit Koppio with shovel, Koppio bin get shovel two fellow pull; Koppio hit Ah Loy on hand, Ah Loy go like this (shows), little fellow Chinaman bin chase em up me, and bin killem shoulder, ribs and hips along shovel, Ah Loy race back and get him gun, put him along shoulder. I go time like this (ducking), big fellow frightened. Koppio bin give me one fellow spear, say "kill em quick fellow before him killem you," I bin hook em up spear and throw him Ah Loy; hit him along back and come out along front. Koppio bin catch em another spear and put him along woomera and kill em little fellow Chinaman.[31]

With that, the defence closed, the jury retired for a short time, then reappeared to announce Katterinyan was guilty – with a rider condemning the practice of the Crown instituting regular rehearsals of the witnesses. Judge Bevan then sentenced Katterinyan to death by hanging.

When Koppio was hanged the very next day, 15 July 1913, Katterinyan must have had no doubt about his future, four months hence.

Three days later, Chief Protector of Aborigines W.G. Stretton wrote to Administrator Gilruth, "humbly" asking his intercession and clemency in Katterinyan's case on the following grounds:

That aboriginals are rendered unaccountable for their actions by the Chinese who give them opium and spirits. The wife of Koppio states that opium and spirits were given to her by Chinese.

That Koppio having suffered the extreme penalty of the law, appeals to your petition are a sufficient vindication of the law.

That a life sentence in this case of Katerinyan [sic] will have a lasting and beneficial effect on the aboriginals generally.

Stretton had clearly changed his mind about the need for execution on country, and:
> ... it was indeed a pitiable experience to note that great effect the execution of Koppio had on all the aboriginals at the Kalin [sic: Kahlin] native village.[32]

Judge Bevan was surprised by the suggestion of the involvement of opium and spirits. This was never mentioned at the trial, and he said that the reference was "quite new," and it was "remarkable that no use was made of it in cross-examination."[33] But he refuted Stretton's comments, concluding that:
> However much one may shrink from the awful nature of capital punishment, there was nothing within the four corners of this case that could warrant me in recommending that the course of justice should be interfered with...[34]

Katterinyan was, he felt, the ringleader in the murder, and there were no extenuating circumstances. He did agree, however, that "humanitarian considerations" were another matter. Despite the urgency of such considerations, four months later Katterinyan was still waiting on death row. Public pressure may have helped. One argument that found traction in the newspapers was a concern about the jury's 'rider' – the condemnation of the practice of testimony rehearsals, where the witnesses were "put through their statements."[35] Even the *Argus* in Melbourne picked this story up,[36] and that led to a Ministerial enquiry.[37] The judge must have tired of the scuttlebutt, and he wrote to the Administrator saying that it was nonsense:
> ... and to single out "murder cases," as apparently has been done, is obviously incorrect, for such practice as exists is common to all cases at which Aboriginal witnesses are concerned.[38]

After Koppio's hanging, a rumble of concern had travelled throughout the community. If Katterinyan had been tried in March, like his friend Koppio, there's little doubt that he would also have been made to climb the gallows steps. His escape and his time on the run saved his life. In November 1913, the readers of the *Herald* were reminded how Koppio, Katterinyan and Anyuana had been arrested for the murder of two Chinese men, and they reported that finally, the government had changed its mind:

> Katterinyan escaped, Anyuana was acquitted, and Koppio was found guilty and hanged… Katterinyan was subsequently recaptured, tried, and sentenced to death…
>
> Mr. Glynn, the Minister for External Affairs, has given close attention to Katterinyan's case, and he has satisfied himself by reading the evidence that he was less culpable than Koppio. Hence the commutation of the death sentence by the Federal Executive today.[39]

But that is not the end of the story. Nine years later, Katterinyan once again escaped from Fannie Bay Gaol.[40] There were three escapees – Katterinyan, Wolgera, and Sugarbag – all 'lifers' locked up for murder.[41] They were at work outside the prison walls and easily eluded the vigilance of a guard named Spriggs to escape into the scrub. Poor Spriggs was later fined £2 (about 3 days' pay) for his negligence.[42]

Wolgera and Sugarbag were recaptured by Mounted Constable Woods a year later, after he received a tip-off and followed them 550 km across the country to Goulburn Island, via Oenpelli. Woods brought them back to Darwin and they were locked up, once again, possibly without further punishment, thought the *Times*, as they were life prisoners.[43]

Katterinyan was from a different part of the Territory, however, and he left the other two to make his way home to the Fitzmaurice River region. Mounted Constable Harry Cameron, of Daly River, was warned of the escape and because he was "a great bushman it is thought that he will most likely intercept them."[44] However, the records are silent as to Katterinyan's fate - he was never heard of again.[45]

Chapter 7: Koppio, 1913

Endnotes

1. *NTTGG*, 5 December 1912, page 3: Terrible Double Murder.
2. Nearly two decades later, Johns wrote a manuscript of his five years in the Territory that was finally published in book form by the Historical Society of the Northern Territory in 1998. See Lewis, 1998.
3. Lewis 1998.
4. Johns, 1913: Katterinyan, Murder, July 14th, 1913, Evidence, NT1913-11019 (Johns, 1913).
5. From Johns' manuscript in Lewis 1998.
6. In Lewis 1998.
7. Napoo was not secured as a witness. Johns needed to move quickly to cross the Daly River before the wet season flood came down, so he had to leave him behind, and he was never seen again. (NT1913-11019, page 3)
8. In Lewis, 1998.
9. *NTTGG*, 23 January 1913, page 3: News and Notes.
10. In Lewis 1998.
11. *NTTGG*, 19 June 1913, Supreme Court.
12. *NTTGG*, 13 March 1913, page 2: Supreme Court.
13. Glynn to Cook, 28 June 1913: NAA: A3, NT 1913/8240 ROLL 7.
14. Carey, 29 March 1913: NAA: CRS A3 NT 1913/8240.
15. Carey, 29 March 1913: NAA: CRS A3 NT 1913/8240.
16. Justice David Bevan, signed by Secretary Carey, 1 April 1913: NAA: CRS A3 NT 1913/8240.
17. Gilruth, 31 March 1913: NAA: CRS A3 NT 1913/8240.
18. Hughes, April 1913: NAA: CRS A3 NT 1913/8240.
19. Hughes, April 1913: NAA: CRS A3 NT 1913/8240.
20. Glynn, 3 July 1913: NAA: A6006, 1913/7/3.
21. Dept. External Affairs memo to Gilruth, 3 July 1913: NAA A6006 1913-7-3 Item 426366.
22. For example, albeit more famous than Koppio, Ned Kelly's execution in 1880 drew a crowd of 5,000 people "composed of a heterogeneous mob of men, women, and children, mainly of the lowest class." *The West Australian*, 23 November 1880, page 3, The Execution of Ned Kelly.
23. *NTTGG*, 17 July 1913.
24. *Townsville Daily Bulletin*, 17 July 1913, page 4: Port Darwin Execution. Aboriginal Murderer.
25. *NTTGG*, 31 July 1913, page 7: News and Notes.
26. NAA: A3 NT1913-11019 pages 4-5.
27. NAA: A3 NT1913-11019 page 6.
28. *NTTGG*, 13 March 1913, page 2: Supreme Court.
29. NAA: A3 NT1913-11019 page 8.
30. Donald Roberts was to become the Judge of the Northern Territory Supreme Court from 1921 to 1928. At just 32 years old, he was the youngest person to have

ever been appointed as a Judge of a Superior Court in Australia. Coincidentally, he was succeeded by the Crown Prosecutor in this case, Ross Mallam, in 1928 (supremecourt.nt.gov.au).

31 NAA: A3 NT1913-11019 page 12-13.
32 Stretton to Gilruth, 18 July 1913, NAA: A3, NT1913/11019.
33 Bevan to Gilruth, 26 July 1913, NAA: A3, NT1913/11019.
34 Bevan to Gilruth, 26 July 1913, NAA: A3, NT1913/11019.
35 *NTTGG*, 31 July 1913, Rehearsals in Court.
36 *Argus*, 15 July 1913.
37 Telegram to Administrator from Department Minister, 16 July 1913, NAA: A3, NT1913/11019.
38 Bevan to Gilruth, 17 July 1913: NAA: A3, NT1913/11019.
39 *Herald*, 5 November 1913, page 8: Aborigine Spared. Life Sentence Passed
40 *NTTGG*, 24 October 1922, page 3: Prisoners Escape.
41 *Northern Miner*, 15 November 1922, page 3: Darwin Notes.
42 *Northern Standard*, 10 November 1922, page 2: Departmental Enquiry.
43 *NTTGG*, 7 August 1923, page 3: Constable's Long Chase.
44 *NTTGG*, 24 October 1922, page 3: Prisoners Escape.
45 Constable Harold Cameron captured 14 escapees between 1919 and 1926 and perhaps Katterinyan was one of these. However, a search for his name, death record, or anything, proved unsuccessful (*NTTGG*, 2 July 1926, page 1: Sensational Capture).

Chapter 8
Jaroslav Koci and Jan Novotny, 1952

Hanged in Fannie Bay Gaol on 8 August 1952, for the murder of George Thomas Grantham.

The Victim

George Grantham was a popular man. Darwin was a small town, and like all small towns, its residents felt they knew everyone. In the years after World War Two, the social pages of the *Northern Standard*, particularly in the column known as *Diana's Diary*, kept readers informed of births, deaths, weddings, parties, arrivals, and departures among the social set of the town.

By 1952, Grantham had been in Darwin for 20 years – having moved north from Port Augusta around 1932.[1] He occasionally appeared in Diana's gossip column, but did so especially on the day he married Dulcie Theresa White in 1948:

> ... for her wedding to Mr. George Grantham, at the Christ Church, Church of England at 6.30 on Sunday evening, Miss Dulcie White chose a charming frock of pale blue Marquisette, draped from the shoulders to the floor, with which she wore a full-length veil of blue held in position with a coronet of orange blossoms.[2]

Dulcie had been a corporal in the W.A.A.A.F. and had arrived in Darwin in 1947. She was a dress maker and a performer who "did a considerate amount of concert work - particularly as a comic singer."[3]

It was a popular wedding. Among the guests were Keith and Rae Jessop. They had started the first taxi company in Darwin, calling it "Jessop's Taxis", and although George Grantham was an independent taxi owner, he had bought the car from Keith. It was a 1950 green Plymouth sedan with licence plate number NT 222. They were competitors, but good friends for nearly 18 years. George and Dulcie had lived with the Jessops for three years after the war, and after Grantham's death, it was Keith Jessop who was called in to identify his body.[4]

Diana's Diary often records the Granthams with other friends at social events:

> Mr. and Mrs. Keith Jessop celebrated their ninth wedding anniversary at the Hotel Darwin this evening. Their guests for dinner were Mr. and Mrs. Grantham, Mr. and Mrs. Fleming, Mr. and Mrs. Barney Lyons, Mr. and Mrs. Delaney, Mr. A. Millard, and Mr. H. Johnson.[5]

The Darwin Taxi-owners' Association was active in those days, and most of the members, like the Granthams, were regular attendees at its annual ball. With as many as 300 guests, these balls were huge affairs in the tiny town. George was also a member of the Royal and Ancient Order of Buffaloes (RAOB), and the Returned Sailors', Soldiers' and Airmen's Imperial League of Australia (RSSAIL – now RSL).[6]

As a driver, Grantham was willing to drive passengers anywhere. "Some drivers have all the luck" wrote Diana in 1948, "George Grantham was seen behind the wheel at Pine Creek."[7]

And in February 1950:

> Darwin taxi-owner George Grantham undertook another of those long-distance fares this week. He drove Molly Daly from Darwin to Tennant where she will be married, and George will take the happy couple across to Mt Isa for their honeymoon.[8]

He was back in Katherine in June – riding a horse named 'Gridiron' in the weekend races:

Chapter 8: Jaroslav Koci and Jan Novotny, 1952

Figure 18: White's Plymouth taxis in Smith Street similar to George Grantham's green Plymouth. The Victoria Hotel is on the right. The water tower in the background is still in use for central Darwin (1950, LANT, ph1117-0012).

Long trip "Jumbo" George Grantham showed the other riders a short cut in winning the Jumbo Stakes on Gridiron.[9]

And then again in July:

Once again "Jumbo" George Grantham of Darwin has visited Katherine. On this occasion the marathon taxi-driver was accompanied by Mrs. Grantham and Mr. and Mrs. Harry Byrnes. George returned the same day. Harry and Mrs. Byrnes are at present staying at the Commercial Hotel.[10]

It was this willingness to drive his passengers everywhere and anywhere that led George to meet two "new-Australians" on 17 April 1952. Jaroslav Koci (aged 20) and Jan Novotny (aged 19) were planning to go home to Czechoslovakia (now the Czech Republic) via Melbourne, and they liked the look of the green Plymouth. They asked Granthem to drive them south, out of Darwin. After just thirteen miles Novotny told him to stop, and while Grantham was talking with Koci, he shot him in the head. Poor Grantham then received two more bullets, shot into his chest to ensure he was dead, and his killers then left his body on the side of the road, next to the Darwin water supply pipes. George was 42 years old.

His friends and the police were soon looking for him and he was found by truckdriver Herbert McDougall, who noticed some tyre tracks turning off the road at the "13-Mile" (This now a light industrial area. The Darwin water supply pipes still run through the place where George was found).

Shocked, McDougall stayed with the body while his wife went to get the police and by 9:30 Sergeant Mutch was on the scene with a photographer named Leslie Lee, who photographed the scene.

His killing was a shock. People knew him across the Territory and sympathy and tributes flowed to his widow, Dulcie, from every town. Angry crowds gathered – given a chance they might have lynched the killers themselves.

Grantham's Funeral

Grantham's funeral was possibly the most well attended in Darwin's history:

> Over ninety vehicles followed the funeral cortege from the Church of England to the Darwin Cemetery last Sunday, when 42-year-old Darwin taxi driver, George Grantham, whose murdered body was found at a lonely spot on the outskirts of Darwin, was laid to rest.
>
> Between four and five hundred people paid their last silent respects as the service was read. A record number of floral tributes gave evidence of the high respect in which the dead man was held.
>
> Members of the Royal and Ancient Order of Buffaloes paid their traditional farewell to their departed friend and comrade.
>
> The *Northern Standard* takes this opportunity of joining the tributes to a popular and well-liked Territorian and expressing deep sympathy with Mrs. Grantham in her bereavement.
>
> Mrs. Grantham has asked that her thanks be expressed to Darwin Taxi Owners, members of the RAOB and the RSS & AILA Club and all relatives and friends for their expressions of sympathy at her great loss.[11]

Chapter 8: Jaroslav Koci and Jan Novotny, 1952

Figure 19: George Grantham's funeral. Dulcie Grantham is dress in black behind the coffin (Photos: Peter Spillett).

The Killers

Grantham's killers were caught on the same day his body was discovered, 19 April. The police put out a BOLOF ("Be On the Look Out For") for Grantham's car, and Sergeant William Simpson and Constable Herbert Hatton had no trouble identifying it, by registration and description, on the unpaved road heading south east from Mount Isa in Queensland.

At first Koci and Novotny, calling themselves Tan Vasely and Milan Tostall, denied any knowledge of the crime. However, when they realised that the Queensland police already knew of the murder, they changed their story.

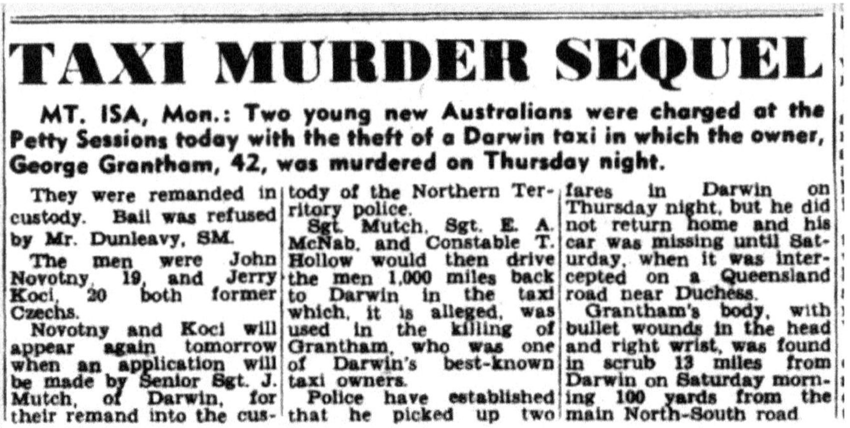

> # TAXI MURDER SEQUEL
>
> **MT. ISA, Mon.:** Two young new Australians were charged at the Petty Sessions today with the theft of a Darwin taxi in which the owner, George Grantham, 42, was murdered on Thursday night.
>
> They were remanded in custody. Bail was refused by Mr. Dunleavy, SM.
>
> The men were John Novotny, 19, and Jerry Koci, 20, both former Czechs.
>
> Novotny and Koci will appear again tomorrow when an application will be made by Senior Sgt. J. Mutch, of Darwin, for their remand into the custody of the Northern Territory police.
>
> Sgt. Mutch, Sgt. E. A. McNab, and Constable T. Hollow would then drive the men 1,000 miles back to Darwin in the taxi which, it is alleged, was used in the killing of Grantham, who was one of Darwin's best-known taxi owners.
>
> Police have established that he picked up two fares in Darwin on Thursday night, but he did not return home and his car was missing until Saturday, when it was intercepted on a Queensland road near Duchess.
>
> Grantham's body, with bullet wounds in the head and right wrist, was found in scrub 13 miles from Darwin on Saturday morning 100 yards from the main North-South road

Figure 20: *NT News*, 21 April 1952, page 1, Taxi Murder Sequel.

When Constable Hatton examined the car, he saw that the driver's seat was stained dark with blood, and there was splatter on the door and windows.

Simpson said that he had:

> ... indicated the car, NT 222, and said, "This car was stolen from Darwin between April 16 and 19 and the dead body of the driver was found near Darwin today. Do you know anything about that?
>
> Both accused replied "No, not know."[12]

They then claimed that two strangers had forced them to drive the car from Mount Isa that morning at gun point, but they had since run away. Simpson and Hatton took them back to a creek where "the strangers" were supposed to have run, but there were no tracks leading either side of the road. Simpson arrested the two Czechs, and kept them overnight in the tiny town of Duchess, before taking them to Mount Isa. Word travelled fast, and within a few hours, Sergeants Verdon Mutch and Eric McNab, and Constable Tom Hollow were on their way from Darwin to interview them.[13]

Koci and Novotny stood in front of Magistrate Dunleavy in Mount Isa's court as soon as they were brought in. Despite their initial claim that they had been forced to drive the car, their lie was easily disproved, as they had been seen buying petrol in Mount Isa. So, by

Chapter 8: Jaroslav Koci and Jan Novotny, 1952

the time they were in court, they were both contrite, and willing to tell the truth – in fact, Novotny was surprisingly candid. He said he was sorry, and his words were later repeated to the jury in Darwin:

> "Koci told the taxi driver to drive us outside the town. After we had been driving from Darwin about ten miles Koci tell him to stop. When he stopped, I shot him in the head. Then we take him from the car out; I caught hold of one hand and Koci caught hold of other hand, and we dragged him into bush. When we get into bush I shoot him again two times. We go back to the car then and Koci drive, and I sit alongside him in front. "

After giving evidence as to the ownership of the murder weapon, Novotny, in reply to a question as to why he bought it, said: "Koci talked to me last Tuesday. He told me he was in trouble over an accident when a little boy was killed. He said it is better we leave here, and you come with me as friend. He said: 'I will get a taxi, and you shoot the driver, and we will go to Victoria and get a ship back to Europe.'"[14]

Koci was equally as forthright:

> "A few days before Novotny shot the taxi driver I said to him: 'I want to leave Darwin and get out of Australia and go back to Europe. I wanted to get away because I couldn't get any chance to play music in Australia.'"[15]

Koci said that after discussing the difficulties of getting to Melbourne or Sydney, Novotny had suggested getting a car and shooting the driver.

"I didn't want to do this," said Koci, "and I told him. This was the day before. I got frightened and I didn't know properly what I was doing."[16]

On the way to Mount Isa, Novotny had told Simpson that he would tell the truth. "I shoot driver with rifle, drag body on road, take car" he said, because they wanted to take the car to Sydney or Melbourne and sell it to get the funds to return to Czechoslovakia.

They each signed confessions in Mount Isa. Later, at the trial, Sergeant Mutch was in the witness box for nearly three hours, reading out their statements and answering questions. Novotny had said:

> We bought a rifle so we could shoot the driver and take his car for no other reason. We meant to shoot the driver after we had gone along the road. I sat in the back of the taxi so he couldn't see me when I shot him. Koci told me to do that. When I shot the driver, he fell against Koci, then we took him into the bush. He did not struggle after the first shot. He was dead. We didn't take the money out of his pockets because we were frightened.
>
> There was blood on my clothes, so after we had gone about 10 miles, I took my shirt off and threw it out the window, then my trousers after that and my shoes after another 8 miles. Next morning Koci changed his clothes.
>
> Before we got to Camooweal I put the rifle in the bush near the road. I did not know the name of the driver. I had never seen him before.[17]

With such honest confessions, the killers were held on remand and extradited back to Darwin – returning as passengers in the same taxi as far as Daly Waters, now driven by Sergeants Mutch and McNab. Remarkably, Mutch managed to find the rifle on the way. It was on Soudan Station, a few metres from the edge of a road, and an Aboriginal man he had picked up at the station easily spotted it from the back seat as they drove past. Novotny identified the rifle as the one he used: "He pointed to a spot between the breech and the back sight and said, "There is blood,"" said Mutch. He also found several .310 bullets.

Then, after driving across the Barkly Tablelands, the Plymouth reached Daly Waters, and the accused were flown to Darwin from the little town's airport:

> Two men were charged at Darwin on Saturday morning with the murder of Darwin taxi driver, George Grantham. The men were Jerry Koci (20) and John Novotny (19). Handcuffed together and shabbily dressed when charged, they were guarded by six members of the police force. Elaborate precautions were taken when the men arrived by air at Darwin. The TAA aircraft in which they and their police escort were travelling from Daly Waters, where they had boarded the plane, pulled up at the end of the runway. The

"YES, I SHOT THAT MAN"
ALLEGED ADMISSION IN N.T. TAXI MURDER CASE

DARWIN, May 6.—"Yes, I shot that man. I am sorry," a New Australian is alleged to have told a police sergeant. The New Australian is John Novotny (19), who, with another migrant, Jerry Koci (20) has been charged with the murder of a Darwin taxi-driver.

The Darwin Coroner (Mr. J. W. Nicholls, S.M.) today opened an inquest into the death of the taximan George Thomas Grantham (42, married) near Darwin, on April 17.

Novotny and Koci were in the Court in custody. They were not represented.

Grantham's body, shot through the head, was found 13 miles from Darwin on April 19.

Sergeant Verdon Mutch, said that there was a five-inch wound on the side of Grantham's face, and a small hole near his left ear.

Mutch said that at Mt. Isa, on April 20, he saw a Northern Territory taxi, No. 222. There were dark stains on the back of the front seat, on the floor behind it, and on the door and windows.

Mutch said he told Novotny about the discovery of Grantham's body, and then said, "What do you call it in your country, if one man shoots another?"

Novotny replied, "Murder."

FOUND RIFLE

Mutch said "If you shot a man in a taxi we would call it murder too. If you did that, you will be charged with murder, and if the Court finds that you murdered this man you can get into serious trouble."

Novotny had replied, "Yes, I shot that man. I am sorry."

Mutch said he left Mount Isa on April 23, in the murdered man's taxi, in company with Sergeant E. A. McNag. Constable T. Hollow, Novotny, and Koci, and a native.

Eight miles from Soudan Station they found a .310 rifle near the roadside, and nearby a cardboard box containing some .310 bullets.

Mutch said both men had admitted it was the rifle they had used to shoot Gratham.

Asked by the Coroner, if they wanted to ask Mutch any questions, Novotny and Koci stood up, shook their heads, and said, "No."

The inquest was adjourned to tomorrow.

Figure 21: "Yes, I shot that man." This story was syndicated in most daily newspapers throughout Australia (Queensland Times, 7 May 1952, page 1).

Figure 22: Sergeants Eric McNab (left) and Verdon Mutch (Fannie Bay Gaol Museum).

prisoners alighted with their police escort and walked to the end of the strip. The aircraft then taxied to the usual interstate passenger bay. The men were taken to a police car which was then driven quickly through the main gate of the airport. An RAAF guard immediately shut the gate.[18]

Jaroslav (Jerry) Koci and Jan (John) Novotny were young men who had experienced Nazi occupation of Czechoslovakia and had escaped the turmoil of post-war recovery. Migrants to Australia, in those days, were called *New-Australians*.

Koci was born in 1932. His mother had died during the war when he was about 10 years old, but his father was still living in Czechoslovakia. Working as a chimneysweep, he was accepted for migration to Australia as an unaccompanied youth in 1949, aged 17. He claimed he was afraid that he would be mobilised into forced labour. Arriving in Australia on 8 October 1949, he worked as a drover in Queensland before arriving in Darwin in January, 1952.[19]

Jan Novotny was born on 4 June 1931, so was a year older

Chapter 8: Jaroslav Koci and Jan Novotny, 1952

Figure 23: A rare photograph of John Novotny (left) and Jerry Koci (right) who were sentenced to death for the murder of taxi-driver George Grantham by Justice Kriewaldt in the N.T. Supreme Court. Sergeant Eric McNab is behind them (Northern Standard, 13 June 1952).

than his friend. His route to Australia was via Germany as a 'political refugee' when he was 16 years old. Nothing is known of his family background in Czechoslovakia, except that he claimed his father died when he was 8, and mother when he was 12. He had worked as a coal miner in Czechoslovakia and in New South Wales as a labourer. He arrived in Darwin, apparently in company with Koci in January 1952.[20]

Both were poorly educated and alone in the world with similar backgrounds, so it is little wonder that they formed an inseparable friendship. In Darwin, they found casual work, ate at cafes, and lived in the Don Hotel. They apparently wanted to play music and were regular and popular visitors to Mrs Georgina Schombacher's music shop.

In March 1952, Koci was involved in an accident with a truck on Vestey's Hill, near where Darwin High School now stands. He was riding a BSA motorbike with an eight-year-old pillion passenger named David Clayton. Koci and Clayton were both knocked unconscious and taken to hospital but, unfortunately, David died the next day.[21]

The police had declared it was an accident, but Koci became convinced he was headed for gaol, and he grew desperate to leave Darwin and go back to his home country.

The Trial

In 1952, the Supreme Court of Darwin was in a converted Sidney Williams Hut erected during World War II. For most of the 1950s it was presided over by Justice Martin Kriewaldt, and it was he, and a 12-man jury, who sat in judgement over Koci and Novotny. There was a lot of interest in the trial's proceedings and spectators crowded the seats at the back of the court.

Both Koci and Novotny admitted their guilt, but their naivety came through in their comments to the judge when they made short statements from the dock.

Chapter 8: Jaroslav Koci and Jan Novotny, 1952

Figure 24: Justice Martin Kriewaldt (NAA A9300 5258124).

Koci said:

"I am 20 years old. My mother died when I was about 10 years old. My father, I hope, is still living in Czechoslovakia. I have no relatives in Australia. I came here when I was 18. I have been on cattle stations and droving in Central Australia until I came to Darwin. I liked that job. I don't like Darwin. I have never done anything wrong before and I would like a chance to go back to the bush work and show that I can be a good Australian citizen, and I will never do this sort of thing again."[22]

There were "murmurs in the court" when Koci made this promise.[23]

Then Novotny made his statement – or rather it was read for him because the jury could not understand his thick accent:

"I am only 19 years old. I did not buy the rifle at Bush's to shoot anyone, but to shoot birds and wallabies. My other rifle was broken. I did not mean to shoot the driver. My father died when I was 8; I lost my mother when I was 12. I came to Australia alone when I was 16 years old. I have no relatives in Australia to help or advise me. I do not like being in towns. I want a job in the country. I have never done anything wrong before, and I would like a chance to go back to the bush work and show that I can be a good Australian citizen, and I will never do this sort of thing again."[24]

Despite admitting to a crime of murder, both the young men

held on to the hope that they would be allowed to head out to work in a remote cattle station after they apologised and promised to be good. Their words were guided by A.B. Newell, the defending counsel provided "for the defence of poor persons" by the government, to evoke sympathy. Newell could find few other avenues of defence.

The evidence against them was damning. Items of their clothing and green rope that was found in Novotny's bedroom at the Don Hotel were also found near Grantham's body; they had been seen in the green Plymouth taxi at Adelaide River, Banka Banka, and Mount Isa; and they were caught driving it near Duchess in Queensland. They had also signed confessions in Mount Isa. Koci also had £30 cash on him. As Grantham's money had not been stolen, this had mostly come from several worthless cheques he had cashed on the journey south.[25]

Mutch read out Koci's statement to the court:

> We went to the Don Hotel and Novotny said, "You go and get taxi now." We knew which taxi we wanted. That day we had been walking in town. We saw this taxi, and we say we will get that one. We both said, "That is a beautiful car. We will take that one."
>
> The driver got out in front of the pictures, and I ran to him and said, "Are you engaged?" He said "no" and he took me to the Don Hotel. Then I went in to get Johnny. A few miles past Qantas Novotny said, "You can stop now." He stopped and as soon as he had stopped, I heard the shot.
>
> He had not switched off the engine and must have straightened his legs when shot. The car started to go again. He had stepped on the gas. I had to straighten the wheel and switch off the engine. I couldn't look at him then and I got out of the car. Novotny called me to help him, and we took the driver into the bush.
>
> When we returned to the car, Novotny said he wanted to make sure the driver was dead. He got the rifle, went back into the bush, and I heard two more shots. Then we drove on. I drove and we were doing between 60 and 70 miles an hour.[26]

The prosecution called 14 witnesses to describe what they

had seen. One of them was the E.W. Bush salesman who had sold Novotny the rifle: Frank Johnston worked at the secondhand dealers, and he readily identified the .310 rifle he had sold on 16 April for £5.[27] Another, Senior Constable Lionel McFarland, had found the clothing and shoes Novotny had thrown out the car window, as well as a cigarette lighter, two .310 cartridge cases, and some green cord used to tie jeans around the rifle.[28] The cord was identical to some he collected in Novotny's hotel room.

There was little that Counsellor Newell could do "except to point to sundry minor discrepancies in the evidence of the witnesses and to attack the voluntary nature of the confession."[29] However, the confessions were both oral and written in lengthy statements, and Judge Kriewaldt accepted them both:

> I have no doubt in my mind that the oral confessions to Detective Sergeant Simpson and the written confessions obtained by Sergeant Mutch of the Northern Territory Police were freely and voluntarily made. I further have no doubt in my mind that those confessions give a substantially true account of the circumstances under which the deceased was murdered.[30]

The judge went on to summarise their confessions, which were materially the same as each other's:

> I think it is a fair summary of the confessions that the two accused decided to return to Europe and that, to procure the necessary money for this purpose, they agreed to steal a motor vehicle with a view to the sale of this vehicle in a southern capital. In my opinion it was part of their agreement that the owner of the vehicle would be killed, and his body hidden.[31]

Kriewaldt carefully explained the law and the duties of the jury. "You take the law from me, and you act upon that," he said, and:

> You and you only are the judges so far as the facts of the case are concerned. The ultimate responsibility of the verdict lies upon you and not me.[32]

Figure 25: The Supreme Court sat in this unairconditioned Sidney Williams hut from 1948-1965.

The Verdict

When the jury retired, they were out for only 24 minutes before returning. This was longer than necessary, according to the *Daily Telegraph*, because afterwards one juryman was quoted as saying:

"We wanted to give our verdict right away but thought we'd do the decent thing and go out for a few minutes. It was a brutal, cold-blooded murder. When we found Koci and Novotny guilty we meant that they should be sentenced to death and the sentence carried out."[33]

Chapter 8: Jaroslav Koci and Jan Novotny, 1952

For this reason, they decided not to give a recommendation for mercy. Justice Kriewaldt agreed with them. Kriewaldt had spent the war years as a squadron leader and later participated in the Japanese war crimes trials, so he was in no mood to contradict the jury. Later in his career, Kriewaldt was increasingly opposed to the death penalty, but at the same time of sentencing the two men he said:

> I agree with the verdict of the jury and with the absence of any recommendation for mercy. Personally, I can see no distinction between the two accused. Novotny, who fired the shot, would seem to be the younger of the two, judging by appearances. Koci, the elder, I judge to be the more forceful character of the two, but this impression is formed only from seeing them in the dock for two days.[34]

Justice Kriewaldt read the death sentence to the two young men:

> "You will be taken from here to Darwin gaol and thence to a place to be named by the Governor-General, to be hung by the neck until you are dead."[35]

According to the *Northern Standard*, Novotny remained calm on hearing his fate, but Koci "showed signs of emotion" as they were led out to a waiting "Black Maria"[36] and driven back to Fannie Bay Gaol[37], from which they thereafter never left. For the next few months, they were held separately from the other prisoners, and they spent their time playing tennis with wooden bats. They were together, but alone in the world:

> They saw no other prisoners, received no mail, and made no effort to write to relatives in Europe.[38]

The long days might have been eased, just a little, by a few luxuries bought for them by the gaolers using the small amount of personal cash they owned when captured. A total of £8.16.9 was spent on "tobacco, fruit and toilet requirements."[39]

NT Administrator approval.

The trial had been a great success. It was of high interest to the population of Darwin, and the courtroom had been crowded

LIST OF PROPERTY IN POSSESSION OF DEFENDANTS, KOCI AND NOVOTNY, WHEN APPREHENDED ON 20th APRIL, 1952.

KOCI:

KOCI: 1 small suitcase;
2 multi-coloured towels;
1 pair of light green swimming trunks;
1 yellow silk tie with diamond pattern;
2 handkerchiefs;
1 studded belt;
1 safety razor, case and razor blades;
1 ~~toothbrush;~~
1 ~~tube toothpaste;~~ } used
1 comb;
1 reel white cotton;
4 needles
1 scroll pen;
1 cigarette lighter, Boss make;
1 Elgy chrome wrist watch, with white plastic wrist-band;
1 hair-brush;
1 tin tan shoe polish;
and an amount of £38/8/1, comprising two £10 bank notes, three £5 bank notes, two £1 bank notes, one 10/- bank note, 10/-d. in silver and 1d. in copper. Also:-
1 green striped sports shirt, gents. *Not Received*

NOVOTNY:

1 yellow silk tie with square pattern;
1 35m.m. Leica camera; *Not Received*
1 Elgy Etanche chrome wrist watch, with chrome wrist band;
1 ~~tooth-brush;~~
1 ~~tube tooth paste;~~ } used
1 ~~comb (wire);~~
1 pair sun glasses; *damaged & destroyed*
and an amount of 16/8¼d., comprising 16/3d. in silver and 5¼d. in copper.
1 white handkerchief

Full sum of money received for John Novotny from sale. 18/8½

for Jerry Koci £7.18"1

The total amount of £8.16.9½ was spent on purchases for the two concerned in Tobacco, Fruit & like requirements.

Figure 26: A list of possessions brought into the gaol by Koci and Novotny (NTRS 3780/P1 1345 Koci, J. (Part 2, page 12)).

throughout the trial. The spectators, we are told by the *Standard*, included "many fashionably dressed women."[40]

Both the guilty men had been children during the tumultuous years of Nazi occupation in Europe and had lived through all the terrors that that involved, and Northern Territory Administrator Frank Wise gave this some thought before approving the young men's executions:

> The two accused are new Australians and the environment in which the greater part of their lives have been spent, should receive consideration. I do not know what evidence was given on this aspect of the matter, but according to press reports the two men are Czechoslovakians and it may be assumed that most of their impressionable years were lived in an atmosphere of disorder, if not lawlessness, and in such circumstances, life would tend to be held cheaply.[41]

Unfortunately for the condemned, Wise may have been swayed by public opinion, which was "and still is, shocked by the circumstances of the crime," he wrote, and:

> … it is important in my view that the decision made in this case should be such as to give satisfaction to the reasonable mind that justice has been done. From my point of view the effect of a judicial execution in a small community and the unfortunate background of the prisoners must be weighed against:
>
> 1) The fact that the jury offered no recommendation for mercy.
>
> 2) The actual circumstances of the crime, and
>
> 3) The need for a penalty that will act as sufficient deterrent.
>
> I feel I must say that the considerations last mentioned outweigh the importance or appeal of those which suggest that the sentences should be commuted. It is recommended, therefore, that the sentence of death be allowed to proceed.[42]

Appeal for commutation

Not everyone agreed, of course, and there were appeals against the sentence. The most rigorous came from a petition for the commutation

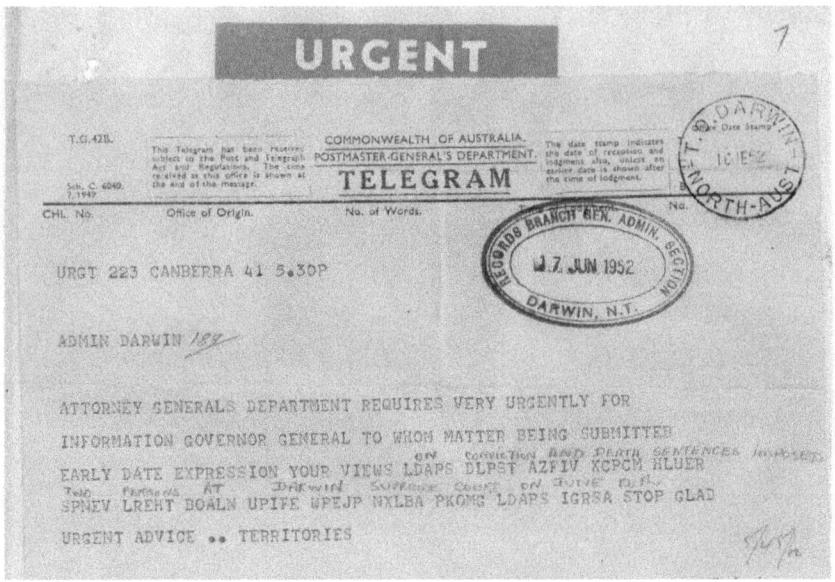

Figure 27: A coded telegram from the Attorney General to the Governor General, 17 June 1952 (NAA F143-S7).

of the sentence from a Czechoslovakian organization in Australia known as the Association of S. S. Cyril and Methodius. They pleaded for a commutation on the grounds that:

(a) Both prisoners were underage at the time of the crime and of their trial.

(b) Both fled from Czechoslovakia at about the age of 16, and since that time they have been lacking any family care, in fact, any care whatsoever during the years most critical in building a character.

(c) Both prisoners came to Australia as teenagers, and, as elsewhere, nobody has taken care of their adequate education and company. They were left alone to shape their own destinies.

(d) While there is no desire to excuse the crime, it appears that the prisoners deserve, not the death penalty, but a period of confinement in a reformatory or penal institute, which is the common solution for juvenile criminals in most civilized countries.[43]

Unfortunately for Koci and Novotny, the association was ignored.

Direction from the Governor-General

The death penalty was serious business, so approval was also necessary from the highest office in the land. Sir William John McKell, a one-time boilermaker-turned union stalwart, lawyer, politician and premier, and then Governor-General, considered the court's ruling and the appeals for commutation carefully, but:

> I, Sir William John McKell, the Governor-General aforesaid, acting with the advice of the Federal Executive on Thursday, 17 April, 1952… have found that… The Administrator of the Territory has reported that the circumstances of the crime do not suggest that a mitigated punishment would be justified. The intention and method of obtaining the motor vehicle which included the killing of its owner appear to have been coldly calculated and planned. The Administrator recommends that the sentence of death be allowed to proceed…
>
> Council do hereby direct that the execution of the sentence of death pronounced by the Supreme Court of the Northern Territory, on the twelfth day of June, one thousand nine hundred and fifty-two upon Jaroslav Koci and upon Jan Novotny be carried into execution within the walls or within the enclosed yard of the gaol at Darwin.[44]

A transfer to South Australia?

At first, the Territory authorities hoped that the execution could be transferred to Adelaide – the Territory had tried this several times over the decades. In 1896, for example, Gaoler George Norcock regularly requested the transfer of long-term prisoners saying their presence was a strain on resources, and they were a security risk. Some prisoners were indeed transferred, but mostly he was ignored.[45]

But in 1952 it was still worth a try. There were no gallows in the Territory in any case, because those used in 1913 had long since rotted away or been eaten by termites. Acting Crown Law Officer Keith Edmunds therefore sent a coded telegram to the Northern Territory's Sheriff Nichols, commanding him to transfer the men to Adelaide.

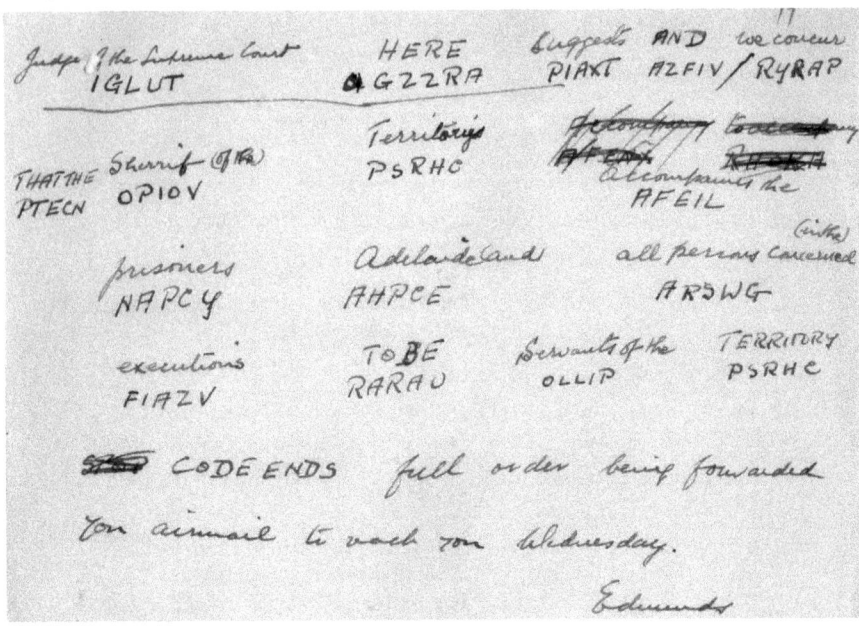

Figure 28: Edmunds' original draft of part of the coded message asking Adelaide if the execution could take place there (NAA: F423 S7).

But a rapid response from South Australian State Crown Solicitor, A.T. Hannon, to Commonwealth Solicitor-General Professor Bailey soon put a stop to that. In a strongly worded refusal that underlined the word 'impossible' twice, Hannon said "that it is impossible to carry out the executions here."[46] Both the Adelaide Gaol and Yatala Prison were full, he said, and by law, South Australian executions could only take place in one wing of Adelaide Prison, and this was at capacity for the foreseeable future. If any executions were to take place there, it meant moving the resident prisoners to other cells – and there were none available.

Hannon's alternative option, after he had consulted his sheriff, was that South Australia could supply the staff and equipment, other than the trap, to the Territory, and that a temporary enclosure could be built at Fannie Bay Gaol. Its wall would need to be 12 feet high, but "a shaft could be dug to give the necessary drop."[47]

There was no alternative, Darwin had to take care of its own execution.

NOW	THESE	ARE	THEREFORE	TO
COMMAND	YOU	THE	SAID	JOSEPH
WESLEY	NICHOLLS	SHERIFF	OF	THE
NORTHERN	TERRITORY	TO	TAKE	AND
CONVEY	THE	SAID	BRACKET	TEXT
RECITES	NAMES	BRACKET	FROM	THE
DARWIN	GAOL	TO	THE	ADELAIDE
GAOL	AT	ADELAIDE	IN	THE
STATE	OF	SOUTH	AUSTRALIA	BEING
THE	PLACE	APPOINTED	BY	THE
LAW	AS	THE	PLACE	OF
EXECUTION	AND	THERE	AT	A
TIME	TO	BE	STATED	BY
THE	SAID	GOVERNOR	GENERAL	TO
HANG	THE	SAID	BRACKET	TEXT
RECITES	NAMES	BRACKET	BY	THE
NECK	UNTIL	EACH	OF	THEM
BE	SEVERALLY	DEAD	ORDER	ENDS
JUDGE	OF	THE	SUPREME	COURT
HERE	SUGGESTS	AND	WE	CONCUR
THAT	THE	SHERIFF	OF	THE
TERRITORY	ACCOMPANY	THE	PRISONERS	ADELAIDE
AND	ALL	PERSONS	CONCERNED	IN
THE	EXECUTIONS	TO	BE	SERVANTS
OF	THE	TERRITORY	CODE	ENDS
FULL	ORDER	BEING	FORWARDED	YOU
AIRMAIL	TO	REACH	YOU	WEDNESDAY
		EDMUNDS		

Figure 29: The full (decoded) message sent to Adelaide commanding relocation of the execution from Darwin, but to be run by Territory public servants (1952, NAA F423, S7).

Report from the Crown Law Office

Thirty-nine years had passed since Koppio was hanged in 1913, so it was a new experience for everyone involved. Acting Crown Law Officer Keith Edmunds took pains to ensure that the execution of the two young men went smoothly. He also recorded the steps taken so that everything learned from the process would be available for use in the future, if needed.⁴⁸

Edmunds described how the gallows were built over a pit dug into the rock beneath the gaol's infirmary – without the use of explosives because of a concern about the building's foundations.

> ...Whilst the excavation was being made, a cover for one end of the hole covering the steps leading to the bottom of the pit was made in one workshop and the trap of the gallows itself was requisitioned for as a heavy man-hole cover in another workshop. The mechanism to control the trap was fabricated in Adelaide and special arrangements were made with T.A.A. to fly this part, which was 14 ft. long, to Darwin. The heavy beam for carrying the ropes was made in Darwin and ordered as part for a crane.⁴⁹

As different parts of the structure were manufactured in different workshops around Darwin, no one knew that gallows were being prepared in the community. Of course, this did not stop the Telegraph from claiming otherwise, after the event:

> In the last days while they waited for news from Canberra on their fate. Koci and Novotny heard strange noises about the jail – hammerings, explosions, hangings. Unknown to them, Darwin's new gallows was being erected. First news the town had about it was when a local contractor began calling at the Parap Hotel for a beer every half hour. He said he was working at the nearby Fanny Bay Jail digging a pit 10 feet deep in the old jail infirmary. It was for a cesspool, he said. The whisper spread around Darwin's 5000 white and colored [sic], public servants, pearl divers, crocodile shooters, and beachcombers. "The lynching is off. They're digging a gallows pit." Two days later the Department of Works engaged 12 men to build a gallows, a hangman's room, and a fence around the jail infirmary.' The job cost £2800. Then an anonymous hangman, two assistants, and a senior Prisons Department official arrived from South Australia. But there was still no official announcement as to whether the murderers would actually be hanged. Koci and Novotny passed away the time playing tennis with each other. They used wooden bats and a tennis ball.⁵⁰

Chapter 8: Jaroslav Koci and Jan Novotny, 1952

The gaol's infirmary building was redesigned to contain two small rooms at one end – on the right was a cell where the condemned would spend their last few hours. The other room was for the executioner to stay in overnight, under guard, before his work was to be done. The dividing wall between them is long gone, but there is a mark on the floor where it once was.

In the meantime, a 12-foot-high metal fence was installed to enlarge the gaol's grounds and enclose the infirmary building – prior to this the building sat outside the gaol fence (see figure 30). To do this, they used explosives to dig the post holes in the rock, so this probably drew attention. However, as the development had been approved prior to the trial, its construction was expected, along with the construction of a solitary confinement cell and the installation of electric washing machines,[51] so it still "did not excite any curiosity."[52]

An expert named Mr Zenker flew in from Adelaide to fix the workings of the gallows, which were based on those of Newgate Prison in England. Zenker had everything running smoothly by 4 August, and "rehearsals were made so that the timing would be exact."[53]

Messrs. Connole, Allen, and Barbier also flew in from Adelaide to help. They were experienced in conducting executions in their state, so could advise the Territorians well. Barbier was even a Roman Catholic, so could help the priest comforting the condemned, as they too were of the faith. With them was a Mr. "Smith", an anonymous hangman who was to be quickly smuggled out of Darwin after the event. The South Australians had to keep a low profile in town and luckily were not recognised by the "southern pressmen" staying at the same hotel.

Koci and Novotny were told that commutation had been refused by the Administrator and the Governor-General on Monday afternoon, 4 August 1952. The next day they were told the execution would take place at 8 a.m. the following Friday.

Arrangements were made. The priest visited the prisoners daily and provided them with a copy of the New Testament in Czech.

Figure 30: Fannie Bay Gaol from the rear in 1930. The infirmary on the left is outside the gaol's wall. (Commercial postcard, LANT ph1168-0007).

The priest agreed to be there before, during, and after the men were hanged, and would hold mass and administer the Last Sacrament and Last Rites. Koci found the time particularly stressful:

> Other prisoners complained that Koci kept them awake all night by chanting a Czech Mass in a high, hysterical falsetto...[54]

A coronial enquiry was necessary immediately after the execution, and Edmunds arranged for Mr. R. L. Odlum J.P., the Acting Principal Legal Officer in the Crown Law Office, to be there for the task. The death warrants were then drawn up ready for his signature. The warrants, wrote Edmunds, are "ultimately endorsed in the margin by the Sheriff and returned to the Judge of the Supreme Court. It is customary for the seal of the Court to be in black wax and for black ribbon to be used."[55]

During the week, two graves were quietly dug and readied within the gaol walls. The police were organised to block traffic along the roads around the gaol for 10-15 minutes at 8 a.m. A local bus, carrying 40 passengers was held up "by devious means" so that by the time it passed the gaol gates, it was running 10 minutes late. None of the passengers knew why – few outside the gaol knew what was

Chapter 8: Jaroslav Koci and Jan Novotny, 1952

> # Darwin's gallows worked in secret
>
> *By a Special Reporter*
>
> **DARWIN, Sat.—Two New Australians hanged here on Thursday did not learn their fate until 24 hours before the time set for their execution.**
>
> The men, Jerry Koci, 20, and John Novotny, 19, both Czechs, were hanged at Fanny Bay Jail, at 8 a.m. on Thursday, for the murder of George Grantham, a Darwin taxi driver.
>
> They were the first white men to be executed in the Northern Territory, and their hanging was a closely guarded secret.
>
> Police openly admitted that they feared a "lynching" attempt by angered Darwin residents who knew and well liked the murderers' victim.
>
> From the time of their arrest in Duchess, Queensland, Koci and Novotny were heavily guarded by armed police.
>
> Police brought the men to Darwin on a secret midnight flight from Daly Waters, and took them to Fanny Bay Jail from the airport's back entrance.
>
> They were segregated from fellow prisoners, and a large force of armed police watched over them constantly.
>
> The murder of George Grantham, one of Darwin's most popular residents, shocked the easygoing Territorians.
>
> On April 17, Koci and Novotny decided to hire a taxi, shoot the driver, than drive to Melbourne, sell the car, and return to Europe.
>
> They wanted to do this, they said, because "we can't play music in Australia."
>
> They "selected" Grantham because his car was an expensive new American model. As Grantham drove them along the Stuart Highway they shot him and dumped his body on the roadside.
>
> Then they drove his car 1200 miles across the Territory to Duchess, Queensland, where police arrested them.
>
> Territorians gathered in pubs and camps all over the Territory to "talk over" the crime and its perpetrators.
>
> Outback police stations telephoned Darwin headquarters, reporting "lynching" threats.
>
> Angered Territorians rode and drove into Darwin from scattered towns and stations.
>
> The atmosphere in Australia's northern "frontier" town grew tense.
>
> The free - and - easy "troppo" Fanny Bay Jail (where prisoners traditionally walk out for a beer, a meal, or a swim and return for "roll-call") became an outback Bastille.
>
> Every new "lynching" rumor alerted armed police guards at the condemned cells and around the flimsy jail walls of corrugated iron and barbed wire.
>
> When Koci and Novotny were finally "smuggled" into town for trial on June 13, the Darwin Supreme Court jury reached its verdict in 24 minutes.
>
> One juryman said afterwards: "We wanted to give our verdict right away, but thought we'd do the decent thing and go out for a few minutes.
>
> "It was a brutal coldblooded murder. When we found Koci and Novotny guilty we meant that they should be sentenced to death and the sentence carried out."
>
> In the last days while they waited for news from Canberra on their fate Koci and Novotny heard strange noises about the jail — hammerings, explosions, bangings.
>
> Unknown to them, Darwin's new gallows was being erected.
>
> First news the town had about it was when a local contractor began calling at the Parap Hotel for a beer every half hour.
>
> He said he was working

...

at the nearby Fanny Bay Jail digging a pit 10 feet deep in the old jail infirmary. It was for a cesspool, he said.

The whisper spread around Darwin's 5000 white and colored public servants, pearl divers, crocodile shooters, and beachcombers.

"The lynching is off. They're digging a gallows pit."

Two days later the Department of Works engaged 12 men to build a gallows, a hangman's room, and a fence around the jail infirmary.

The job cost £2800. Then an anonymous hangman, two assistants, and a senior Prisons Department official arrived from South Australia.

But there was still no official announcement as to whether the murderers would actually be hanged.

Koci and Novotny passed away the time playing tennis with each other. They used wooden bats and a tennis ball.

They saw no other prisoners, received no mail, made no effort to write to relatives in Europe.

One day last week a Roman Catholic priest arrived at the jail with a New Testament in Czech.

He left it with the prisoners. After that he visited them each day

A warder told them they could have as many cigarettes as they wanted, any special food.

The daylight chatter of the "free" prisoners outside the condemned cells became a confusion of hushed murmurs.

Koci and Novotny began to fear the worst. Koci was the first to break.

Other prisoners complained that Koci kept them awake at night by chanting a Czech Mass in a high hysterical falsetto

Then, last Monday, the Executive Council met in Canberra and gave the final decision. Koci and Novotny must hang.

On Tuesday the news was known in Darwin, on Wednesday the Czechs learned their fate.

On Thursday at 9.30 a.m. the Northern Territory Administrator, Mr. P. J. Wise, called a Press conference and announced that Koci and Novotny had been hanged at 8 a.m.

"All precautions," he said, "were taken to ensure that the executions were carried out in accordance with the requirements of a small population such as Darwin's."

But by that time all Darwin knew the killers had been hanged.

RESIDENTS of Fanny Bay suburb awoke that morning and found the roadway in front of the jail cordoned off and heavily guarded by armed police.

Other police patrolled the long, sandy beach over which Fanny Bay jail looks at the Timor Sea.

A little knot of residents gathered near George Grantham's house, a stone's throw from the jail walls.

At 8 a.m. the guards looked at their watches, everybody knew what that meant.

There was no further need to talk "lynching" in the pubs.

The Territory is not sorry that it can no longer boast: "No white man will ever hang here."

The authorities erected gallows in Darwin once before—in 1913 to hang a half-caste

The termites ate that gallows, but the new one has been "white ant proofed".

It's there to stay. Darwin authorities believe the Federal Government will in future use Darwin as the official "execution centre" for all Commonwealth Territories.

. . . A JURY VOTED FOR DEATH

Figure 31: *The Daily Telegraph*, 10 Aug 1952.

happening within its walls.

Koci and Novotny were awakened at 5:30 a.m. on the morning of their last sunrise. They dressed in their ordinary clothes and were taken to the cell built especially for them at the rear of the infirmary.

As they entered, they had their first view of the gallows on their left. They were then given breakfast. The hangman, under guard in the cell next door, waited with the trap mechanism. He could hear the condemned in their final hours through the thin brick wall and would have listened as the priest arrived to conduct a religious ceremony for the condemned men at 7 a.m., and to their last conversations.

Then, a few minutes before eight, the prisoners were strapped by the wrists and shoulders and led the few paces to the gallows. Their ankles were tied, nooses were placed around their necks, and white hoods over their heads. Because they were Roman Catholics, the nooses were in place *before* the hood, noted Edmunds, so that the priest could anoint the condemned person immediately he dropped, as "otherwise it means cutting away the hood."[56]

The Execution

The official party came in from the gaol office at exactly 8 o'clock. Koci and Novotny were on the trap and ready. Once all in, the sheriff signalled the hangman through the door of his room, and he released the mechanism.

Instantly, and together, Koci and Novotny dropped to their deaths and were immediately "each, severally dead."[57]

The officials then returned to the office. The bodies were left hanging until 9 a.m. when the medical officer pronounced life extinct, and the coroner held his enquiry and ordered that the bodies be buried. Knowledge of the location of their graves has been officially lost, but two plaques on the infirmary wall mark their initials and the date of their execution. Leo Izod, who was 18 years old at the time, believes that the graves are, in fact, under the plaques.[58] He might be right – the graves were ready for the bodies that morning and it would make sense that they were dug through the rock using the same equipment as used for the gallows pit.

The hangman, whose identity remains unknown, was smuggled out of the gaol immediately after the execution and flown back to

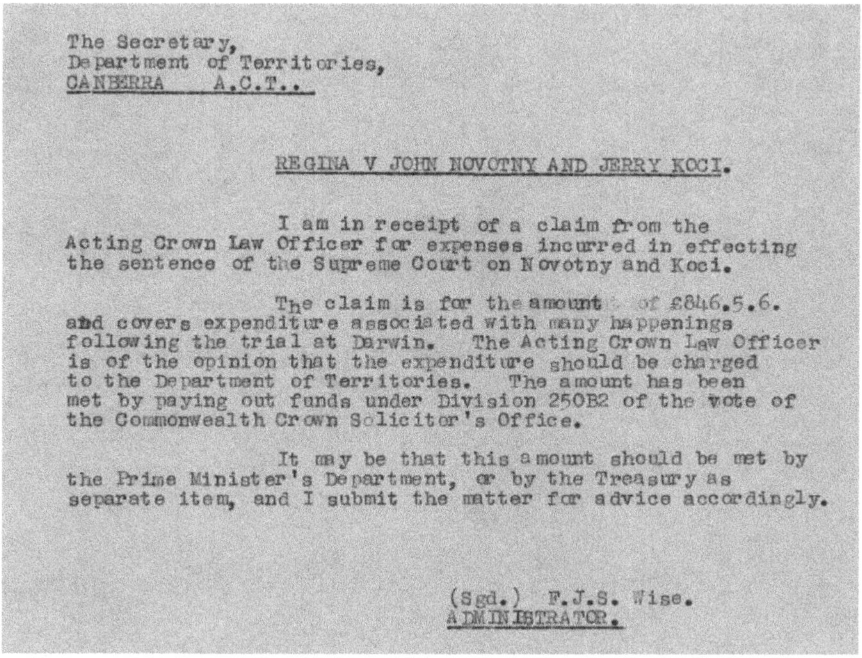

> The Secretary,
> Department of Territories,
> CANBERRA   A.C.T..
>
> REGINA V JOHN NOVOTNY AND JERRY KOCI.
>
> I am in receipt of a claim from the Acting Crown Law Officer for expenses incurred in effecting the sentence of the Supreme Court on Novotny and Koci.
>
> The claim is for the amount of £846.5.6. and covers expenditure associated with many happenings following the trial at Darwin. The Acting Crown Law Officer is of the opinion that the expenditure should be charged to the Department of Territories. The amount has been met by paying out funds under Division 250B2 of the vote of the Commonwealth Crown Solicitor's Office.
>
> It may be that this amount should be met by the Prime Minister's Department, or by the Treasury as separate item, and I submit the matter for advice accordingly.
>
> (Sgd.) F.J.S. Wise.
> ADMINISTRATOR.

Figure 32: for a while, there was confusion as to whom would pay the costs of the execution (Wise: NAA, F423, S7).

Adelaide. No-one else was permitted to leave until after the enquiry. However, as Edmunds had been told that it was a long-established custom for the officials to have a drink afterwards, they at least had something to do. Edmunds purchased a bottle of whisky for the use of the official party to settle their nerves.

They probably needed it. Nola Smith's father had been one of the witnesses. In 1995, she told historian Mickey Dewar that he had been sick for days after the execution.[59]

The Cost

The whiskey cost £2.8.0. It was added to the bill for the execution, and when everything was tallied up, the total cost was £846.5.6 (about $20,000 in today's money). For a while, no one was sure which department should pay, but eventually Northern Territory Administrator Wise claimed it back from 'Division 247/C2: Maintenance of Prisons'.

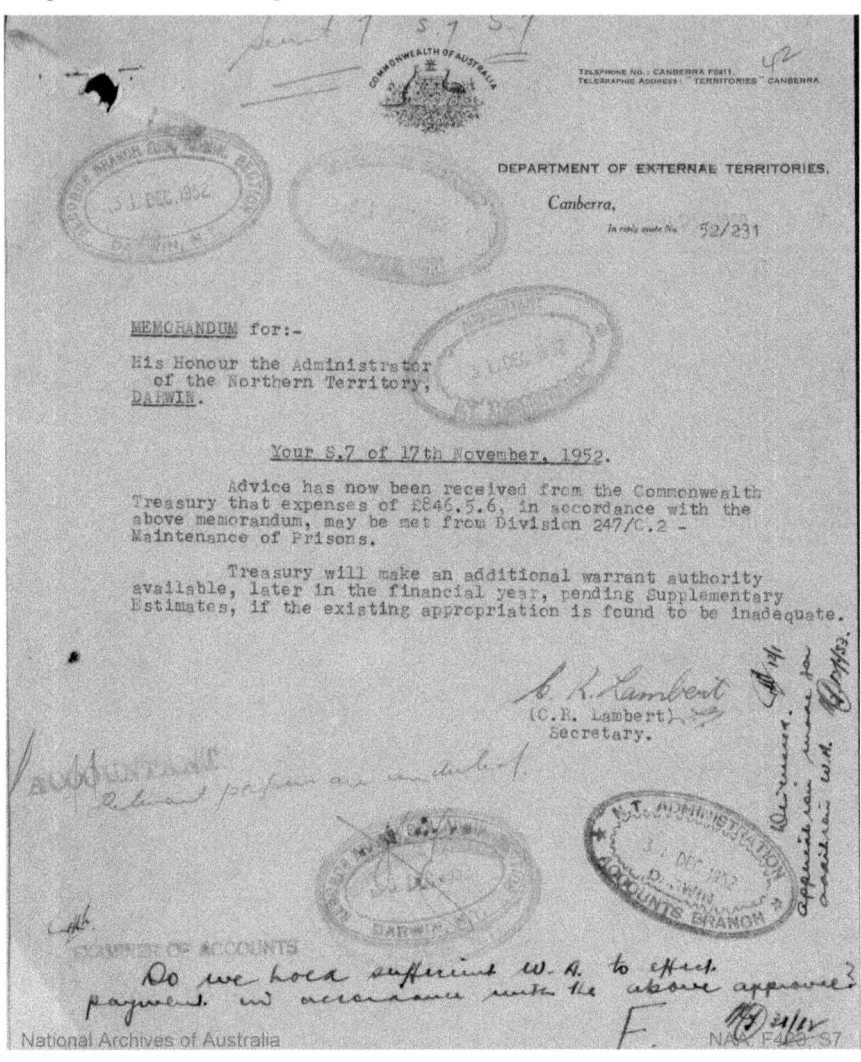

Figure 33: The cost of the execution was £846.5.6. This included £2.8.0 for a bottle of whiskey for the witnesses.

The Revelation

The only thing left to do then was to inform the public that the execution had taken place:

> … at 9.30 a.m. the Northern Territory Administrator, Mr. F. J. Wise; called a Press conference and announced that Koci and Novotny had been hanged at 8 a.m. "All precautions," he said, "were taken to ensure that the executions were carried out in

Chapter 8: Jaroslav Koci and Jan Novotny, 1952

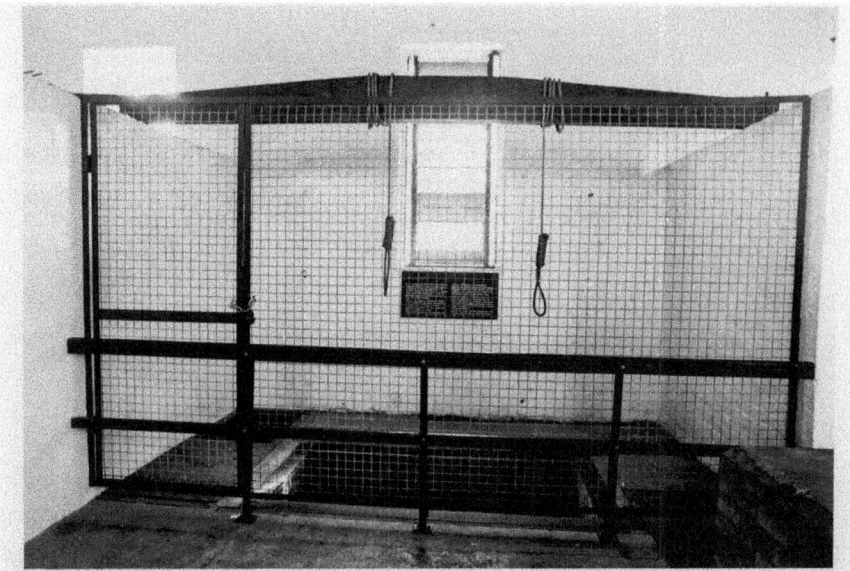

Figure 34: Noose ropes and trap, Fannie Bay Gaol in the 1980s. The ropes are no longer displayed (1983, LANT 10571).

accordance with the requirements of a small population, such as Darwin's."[60]

The Infirmary

That the infirmary building still stands with the gallows inside is a testament to superstition, rather than any heritage minded prison officers. The building has what Mickey Dewar termed a 'cultural legacy'[61] and, as both the prisoners and the staff were superstitious, none of them wanted to be inside it after dark. It "was the old hangman's place…" and useless for accommodation because prisoners would "start complaining that they couldn't sleep because of the ghost in there."[62]

Similarly, the building was useless for adult education programs, as some prisoners would refuse to enter it for any reason at all. It therefore became a storeroom without any remodelling and remained so until the gaol closed in October 1980. The result of the enforced 'non-use' is that Koci and Novotny now have a room in the Fannie Bay Gaol Museum dedicated to their tragic memory.

Endnotes

1. *Quorn Mercury*, 24 April 1952, page 2: Murdered Taxi Driver Was Known in Port Augusta.
2. *Northern Standard*, 9 April 1948, page 10: Diana's Diary.
3. *Northern Standard*, 28 March 1947, page 7: Diana's Diary.
4. *Northern Territory News*, 12 June 1952, page 1: Sentences of death for two men in taxi murder.
5. *Northern Standard*, 10 February 1950: Diana's Diary.
6. Now the RSL.
7. *Northern Standard*, 16 January 1948, page 3: Diana's Diary.
8. *Northern Standard*, 12 May 1950, page 4: Diana's Diary.
9. *Northern Standard*, 16 June 1950, page 10: News from Katherine.
10. *Northern Standard*, 28 July 1950, page 8: Around the Territory.
11. *Northern Standard*, Friday 25 April 1952, page 1: Murder Victim's Funeral.
12. *Northern Territory News*, 12 June 1952, page 1: Sentences of death for two men in taxi murder.
13. *Courier-Mail*, 7 May 1952, page 3: Alleged Taxi Murder Admission.
14. *Northern Standard*, 13 June 1952, page 1: Taxi Murderers to Die.
15. *Northern Standard*, 13 June 1952, page 1: Taxi Murderers to Die.
16. *Northern Standard*, 13 June 1952, page 1: Taxi Murderers to Die.
17. *Northern Territory News*, 12 June 1952, page 1: Sentences of death for two men in taxi murder.
18. *Centralian Advocate*, 2 May 1952, page 1: Koci & Novotny Charged with Murder.
19. NAA: A432, 1952/1490 Part 2, page 3.
20. NAA: A432, 1952/1490 Part 2, page 4.
21. *Northern Standard*, 5 April 1952, Page 3: Victim Dies Child Accident.
22. Report by the Presiding Judge: NAA, F423 S7.
23. *Northern Standard*, 13 June 1952, page 1: Taxi Murderers to Die.
24. Report by the Presiding Judge: NAA, F423 S7.
25. This money went into a police trust account and eventually found its way back to those who had given Koci the cash. R.R. Fretwell of Tennant Creek was paid £20 and T.E. Humphries of Daly Waters, and Max Schober of Newcastle Waters, were paid back £10 each from the trust account in October 1957, five years after the hanging (NTRS 3780/P1 1345 Koci, J. (Part 1)).
26. *Northern Territory News*, 12 June 1952, page 1: Sentences of death for two men in taxi murder.
27. *Northern Territory News*, 9 May 1952: Taxi Owner Inquest: Police Tell of Finding Gun.
28. *Northern Territory News*, 12 June 1952, page 8: Sentences of death for two men in taxi murder.
29. Report by the Presiding Judge: NAA, F423 S7.
30. Report by the Presiding Judge: NAA, F423 S7.
31. Report by the Presiding Judge: NAA, F423 S7.

32 Kriewaldt 1952, Summing up for the Jury.
33 *Daily Telegraph*, 10 August 1952, page 40: Darwin's gallows worked in secret.
34 Report by the Presiding Judge: NAA, F423 S7.
35 *Northern Standard*, 13 June 1952, page 1: Taxi Murderers to Die. Kriewaldt was not a supporter of capital punishment. His biographer wrote that Kriewaldt was shocked by the executions, and they reaffirmed his resolve as a campaigner against the death penalty (Elder, 2008). During his 9 years on the bench in Darwin, Kriewaldt presided over 39 murder trials – none of which ended in execution other than the two Czechs.
36 A "Black Maria" was a name given to police vans used to transport prisoners. It may have been nearly new, as a new Black Maria was spotted in Alice Springs on the way to Darwin in 1951 (*Centralian Advocate*, 9 February 1951, Page 7: New "Black Maria" For Darwin).
37 *Northern Standard*, 13 June 1952, page 1: Taxi Murderers to Die.
38 *Daily Telegraph*, 10 August 1952, page 40: Darwin's gallows worked in secret.
39 (NTRS 3780/P1 1345 Koci, J. (Part 2, page 12)).
40 *Northern Standard*, 13 June 1952, page 1: Taxi Murderers to Die.
41 F.J.S. Wise, Administrator, *Recommendation for execution to proceed*: NAA: F423, S7.
42 F.J.S. Wise, Administrator: NAA: F423, S7.
43 NAA: A432, 1952/1490 PART 2.
44 NAA: A432, 1952/1490 PART 2.
45 Norcock, 1895.
46 A.T. Hannon to Professor Bailey, 7 July 1952: NAA, F423, S7.
47 A.T. Hannon to Professor Bailey, 7 July 1952: NAA, F423, S7.
48 Edmunds, Crown Law Office, 7 August 1952: NAA, F423, S7.
49 Edmunds, Crown Law Office, 7 August 1952: NAA, F423, S7.
50 *The Daily Telegraph*, 10 August 1952, Page 40: Darwin Gallows Worked in Secret.
51 See King: NAA: F1, 1951/647 Part 2.
52 Edmunds, Crown Law Office, 7 August 1952: NAA, F423, S7.
53 Edmunds, Crown Law Office, 7 August 1952: NAA, F423, S7.
54 *Daily Telegraph*, 10 August 1952, page 40: Darwin's gallows worked in secret.
55 Edmunds, Crown Law Office, 7 August 1952: NAA, F423, S7.
56 Edmunds, Crown Law Office, 7 August 1952: NAA, F423, S7.
57 NAA, F423, S7.
58 Leo Izod, personal communication 2 August 2025.
59 Dewar, 1999, quoting an interview with Nola Smith in 1995.
60 *Daily Telegraph*, 10 August 1952, page 40: Darwin's gallows worked in secret.
61 Dewar, 1999.
62 J. Dewsnip, 1994, Transcript of an interview recorded in Fannie Bay Gaol, MAGNT, 11 May. In Dewar, 1999.

Chapter 9
The Science of Execution

During the nineteenth century, South Australia and the Northern Territory, as a colony, operated under British legal customs and principles. The lawmakers of the time often regarded themselves as enlightened and humane, particularly in matters of capital punishment. While some voices called for its abolition, the prevailing view held that capital punishment remained a necessary deterrent for serious crimes, despite the lack of evidence supporting its effectiveness in preventing future offences.

British and colonial authorities sought the most humane methods available for carrying out executions and they had settled on hanging. Unfortunately, not all hangings were equal, and techniques evolved throughout the nineteenth century to improve their humanity. The principal methods included the pole, short-drop, standard, and long-drop hangings. These contrasted in their causes of death — it was either by slow strangulation or by a cervical fracture.

The pole method of hanging was used ruthlessly during the First World War in Eastern Europe, but not by the British. Its major advantage was that it could hang as many people as there were three-metre poles available. Called *Würgegalgen* ("strangling gallows') in Hungary and Czechoslovakia, the method involved tying the condemned high up on the pole by a rope around his or her chest, and a noose around his or her neck, and then releasing the chest support. The condemned would die of strangulation.

The short-drop method was probably the most commonly used throughout history, and it was certainly the usual in Australia for most of the nineteenth century. In the short drop, the condemned person stood or sat on a raised support, such as a stool, ladder, cart, or horse with a noose around his or her neck. As in Western movies, the support was moved away and victims then dangled from the rope, kicking their feet uselessly as their body weight tightened the noose around their necks as they were strangled. Variations had the victims lynched by hauling them off their feet by a rope over a tree branch or similar. Using this method, death was inevitable, but it took a few minutes.

The advantage of these methods was that each corpse was left without mutilation, so they were relatively clean and bloodless. The British in Victorian England however, deemed them cruel. The final seconds and minutes of those hanged were excruciating for the victims and distressing to prison governors and others who were required to witness the executions at close quarters.

The 'standard-drop,' where prisoners would fall four to six feet, was designed to break the prisoners' necks and kill them instantaneously. Unfortunately, it was not always successful and sometimes proved messy if the prisoner's head tore off, or stressful for all concerned if the prisoner lingered through strangulation.

Then came William Marwood (1818-1883), whose aim was to ensure that the prisoners' necks were reliable broken instantly at the end of the drop in a way that death was instantaneous and without mess. The long-drop method was introduced across Britain after he proved its worth on 1 April 1872. On that day, he hanged William Horry so cleanly and efficiently that he was immediately appointed as the official hangman to London and Middlesex, earning a salary of £20 a year, plus £10 per execution.

As the skill in hanging a prisoner was refined, hangmen who could ensure their efforts avoided torture became relatively well-paid public servants - it could not be done efficiently by just anyone.

Chapter 9: The Science of Execution

Figure 35: Executioner James Berry.

Marwood's successor, James Berry (1852-1913) promoted the long-drop method through accurate mathematics in an aim to further diminish mental and physical suffering. His expertise saw 131 prisoners hanged during his seven-year career, including 7 women.[1] Using three-quarter inch, five-strand, Indian hemp rope, he would measure a person's height and weight and accurately calculate how much rope was needed. Too little rope would lead to death by strangulation, too much meant a longer drop, a greater speed, and cut jugulars or worse. Hangmen needed to know how to place the rope, so the prisoner's head would be jerked back as the rope tightened to help break the neck.

Berry described the process he used in his 1892 autobiography, *My Experiences as an Executioner*.[2] Executioners like Berry did not use the knot known as 'the hangman's knot.' Rather, the rope had "a one-inch brass ring worked into one end, through which the other end of the rope is passed to form the noose."[3]

Berry was happy to describe how he executed people in detail:

A leather washer which fits the rope pretty tightly, is used to slip up behind the brass ring, in order to prevent the noose slipping or slackening after it has been adjusted.

In using the rope, I always adjust it with the ring just behind the left ear. This position I never alter, though of course, if there were any special reason for doing so, for instance, if the convict had attempted suicide and were wounded on the side of the throat, death could be caused by placing the ring under the chin or even behind the head. The position behind the ear, however, has distinct advantages and is the best calculated to cause instantaneous and painless death, because it acts in three different ways towards the same end. In the first place, it will cause death by strangulation, which was really the only cause of death in the old method of hanging, before the long drop was introduced. Secondly, it dislocates the vertebra, which is now the actual cause of death. And thirdly, if a third factor were necessary, it has a tendency to internally rupture the jugular vein, which in itself is sufficient to cause practically instantaneous death.[4]

Unfortunately, even Barry's expertise was not foolproof. In 1885 he executed Robert Goodale, a 96kg (15 stone) wife-murderer, in what became known as the *Goodale Mess*. Poor Goodale was decapitated by the rope:

The whole of the arrangements were carried out in the usual manner, and when I pulled the lever the drop fell properly, and the prisoner dropped out of sight. We were horrified, however, to see that the rope jerked upwards, and for an instant I thought that the noose had slipped from the culprit's head, or that the rope had broken. But it was worse than that, for the jerk had severed the head entirely from the body, and both had fallen together to the bottom of the pit. Of course, death was instantaneous, so that the poor fellow had not suffered in any way; but it was terrible to think that such a revolting thing should have occurred. We were all unnerved and shocked. The Governor, whose efforts to prevent any accident had kept his nerves at full strain, fairly broke down and wept.[5]

Berry's methods and data tables were used in the major Australian gaols, but mistakes were sometimes made. The Queensland executioner, William Ware, for example, probably tried to follow Berry's tables closely, but things went horribly wrong, at least once. Wearing his customary hood and fake grey beard to avoid being recognised, Ware hanged Queensland's only female condemned murderer, Ellen Thomson, on 13 June 1887. She was a small woman who weighed just 47 kilograms (less than 7 stone not including the weight of her head), so she was too light to register on the tables.

Chapter 9: The Science of Execution

Unfortunately, Ware miscalculated. He made the rope too short and when Ellen dropped, blood immediately soaked the white hood that had been placed over her head. Her jugular had been cut by the rope and, although she probably died quickly enough, the mess shocked the onlookers, and Ware felt he had failed in his duty.[6]

Length of drop, in feet, is found by dividing the number 539 by the sqaure of the number of stones in weight of convict's body, exclusive of the weight of his head. Thus, if a convist weighs 11 stones altogether, and we take his head as 1 stone, we have length of drop = 539/100 = 5.39 feet (5ft. 5 in. nearly.

Weight of body without head.	Lenght of drop.
15 stones	2 ft. 5 in.
14 stones	2 ft. 9 in.
13 stones	3 ft. 2 in.
12 stones	3 ft. 9 in.
11 stones	4 ft. 6 in.
10 stones	5 ft. 5 in.
9 stones	6 ft. 8 in.
8 stones	8 ft. 3 in.
7 stones	11 ft. 0 in.

From James Berry's *My Experiences as an Executioner* (1892 - p38). After the condemned are weighed (less the weight of the head) the correct rope length can be read from the tables Berry had laboriously worked out through gruesome experience.

For a successful execution, the hangman wanted the neck to be broken quickly with no other effects other than death. The record speed in Britain was just seven seconds from the executioner entering the cell to the drop. The hanging of Koci and Novotny in Darwin in 1952 might have been almost as quick, because the executioner was waiting next to the gallows, ready to pull the lever as soon as the prisoners were in place. Plus, he was an experienced man, specially brought up from Adelaide.

Efficiency and Method in Historical Executions

The government and press reports always assured the public that the executions in the Northern Territory ended in 'instantaneous' deaths. However, when Sheriff John Little selected his hangmen from the willing prisoners wanting to earn early release from the gaol, he was not choosing men from a pool of well trained and knowledgeable hangmen. None of them would have read Berry's book, so it is doubtful that these executions matched the efficiency of the events in 1952 – except by chance. Flannigan was said to have provided his hangman with advice on how to tie the knot, and the six feet of rope used for his execution appeared to work effectively, but this success may have had little to do with the expertise of the hangman.

There is no record of any prisoners being accidentally decapitated, so indeed, the fortunate may have been hanged efficiently, but there remains the possibility that some were strangled in the short-drop tradition. The executioners might not have reported such mistakes.

Endnotes

1. Wade, 2009.
2. James Berry, 1892: *My Experiences as an Executioner.*
3. James Berry, 1892: *My Experiences as an Executioner.*
4. James Berry, 1892: *My Experiences as an Executioner.*
5. James Berry, 1892: *My Experiences as an Executioner.*
6. Farrer, 2014.

Hanged: Execution in the Top End

Chapter 10
Epilogue

The death penalty was never popular in the Northern Territory, and most judges were loath to give it. When it was given, and there has always been plenty of murderers, it was usually commuted to life imprisonment. For example, in his annual report, Warden A.G. Strath claimed that 1913 was an unusually active year for murderers:

> During the year there has been an unusual number of aboriginal native prisoners brought to prison charged with murder. Thirteen prisoners – twelve aboriginal natives and one European – were brought to trial at the supreme court. Seven were found guilty and sentenced to death. One was executed, and six were afterwards commuted to imprisonment for life with hard labour. Five were found not guilty, including one European. One aboriginal native is at present awaiting trial.[1]

The Aborigines who came before the courts, chained and manacled as they were, might have appeared particularly pitiful. Defence Counsel H. A. Shierlaw defended many people in the Palmerston court as a young man. In 1934 he was asked for his opinion about the process of trying Aboriginal men and their terror at the process. He recalled the trial of Cumbit and Donghol in Palmerston, whom he had defended in Palmerston in 1905. These two "myall blacks" had murdered Fred Bradshaw and Ivan Egelhof in 1905:

> … It was well known in the north that natives captured for an alleged serious offence were prostrated with terror when they were brought into court manacled and chained, he said. The sense of lost freedom completely overwhelmed them… when

the three men, heavily chained, were brought into court by the police they lost all control.[2]

It was possibly the judges' sympathy when watching the accused, combined with growing public opinion and political influence, that kept the death penalty mostly at bay. When juries recommended mercy, the death penalty was always commuted. Whatever the reason, it certainly worked, because it was another 39 years until it was used again in the Territory, and that was for Koci and Novotny, two very different characters from the murderers of the turn of the century.

Capital punishment was banned in the Northern Territory in 1973, following the lead of the Federal Government. Australia had inherited the penalty from the British at settlement, and in the 19th century about 80 people were hanged each year for crimes such as burglary, sheep stealing, forgery, sexual assaults (including sodomy), murder, and manslaughter.[3] The ten men hanged in the Territory were all found guilty of murder.

Most of the criminals who were hanged across Australia are mostly forgotten - the exception being a few high-profile criminals such as Ned Kelly, and Ronald Ryan (as he was the last). Novotny and Koci are remembered in the Territory because the gallows, and the infirmary within which they were built, are now a part of the gaol museum.[4]

Visitors can read the information about the two Czechs, and peer down into the pit and wonder about the events that took place so secretly there at 8 a.m. on 7 August 1952. During the gaol's early years as a museum, two rope nooses hung from the beam, seemingly ready for their next customers, in a macabre display of poor taste. They were never used, of course, and have long since been removed to make the modern experience of visiting the gallows less gruesome. In fact, for most people, it appears to be an experience that lacks emotion.

Nevertheless, there are people still living in Darwin who recall the excitement the murder and the double execution caused in the

Figure 36: George Grantham's grave lies just near the entrance gate of the Gardens Hill Cemetery. In what was the largest funeral procession that had been seen in Darwin, five hundred people followed the hearse to the cemetery for his internment, in April 1952. In George's memory, Dulcie arranged a solid granite headstone for his grave with help from "all his mates." Its letters are now fading, and no one has left flowers in the receptacles provided for many years. Dulcie, and George's mates, are themselves long gone.

community in 1952. Ninety-one-year-old Leo Izod remembered it well. "It was the horror of it," he said in 2025. "Nothing like that had ever happened before, you see… everyone was talking about it, the horror."[5]

They were still talking about it in 1956 when John Flynn arrived in Darwin. "Everyone knew all about it. Everyone had an opinion. We heard about it as soon as we arrived" he said.[6]

Complaints about the prison and the treatment of its prisoners were heard for decades. For example, Charles Priest was unfortunate enough to spend a few days in the gaol in June 1932. Although June is a cool month for the steamy north, he was still critical of the gaol's design:

> The cells are badly ventilated and even in cold weather the prisoners emerge from their cells semi-stupefied each morning though breathing the same air over and over again.[7]

Figure 37: H. M. Gaol and Labour Prison, Darwin (aka Fannie Bay Gaol) is now a museum.

Figure 38 [Left]: the trap mechanism - when the lever was pushed to the left, the trap door opened and the condemned fell to their deaths. It was only used once. Figure 39 [Right]: The Fannie Bay Gaol gallows. The executioner waited unseen in the room with the trap mechanism. The wall between him and where the prisoners were prepared has been removed, but it is still marked on the floor.

Figure 40: the Fanny Bay Gaol gallows - once noosed and hooded, Koci and Novotney fell into this pit. Their necks were broken instantly. They were left hanging while the coroner completed his report and at 9 a.m. the bodies were released and were taken to their graves.

Figure 41: The location of Novotny and Koci's graves has been officially lost, but two plaques on the infirmary wall mark the date of their execution.

Prisoners on remand were hardly any better off, despite not having criminal convictions. There was nowhere to keep them, apart from the corridor, and they were not allowed outside:

> All [remand] prisoners, whether black, white, or yellow, are kept in the corridor while awaiting trial," [Superintendent] Mr. Walker said. "They are allowed out once a day for a bath but are not allowed in the yard where other prisoners are working because they would cause interruptions and disorganisation.[8]

In 1953, Douglas Lockwood was particularly scathing in a report he wrote just months after Novotny's and Koci's last days. He spent two hours in Fannie Bay Gaol and wrote that it was "a disgrace to the entire Australian prison system." The gaol was far worse than he imagined, he said, and it deserved to be demolished:

> When I visited the gaol, 35 prisoners were sharing 16 cells. Four of these men had to be segregated, so there were only 12 cells for 31 prisoners.
>
> Each cell is 12 ft. square. There are three men in most of them, but one contains six natives. There is no room for beds, so they all sleep on mats on the concrete floor, their feet touching in the centre. The stench is unbelievable. All the cells are scrubbed daily with disinfectant, but nothing the staff and

prisoners can do will eliminate the overpowering stench. What it is like in these cells at night can only be guessed.

The prisoners live in what is almost a Turkish bath. After five minutes in one cell with the iron door open – it is closed at night – my hands, arms and face were dripping. The only ventilation is an aperture near the ceiling, too small to admit any breeze. Because of mosquitoes the prisoners have to sleep under nets. This raises the temperature considerably. It was these circumstances which prompted a senior public servant to say last week, "It's a wonder some prisoners haven't attempted suicide or gone crazy." In fact, one prisoner has attempted suicide twice recently.

There is no hospital or isolation block for prisoners with infectious diseases. They all eat together in the entrance vestibule to the cell block. I asked one old man if he could sleep at night. "You can't sleep in that heat," he said. "You are lying in a pool of perspiration from the moment you enter the cell until you are released next day."[9]

The Fannie Bay Gaol, formally called *Her Majesty's Gaol and Labour Prison*, was emptied in 1979 and closed for good in 1980, after 97 years of service. The prisoners were moved to a larger, more modern, facility at Berrimah, on the outskirts of Darwin.

Fannie Bay Gaol as a Museum

In 1982, the former prison facility was transformed into a museum. Initially railway engines and carriages were also displayed on the site, offering visitors a broader glimpse into the region's history. However, these exhibits have since been removed, and the focus has returned solely to the gaol itself.

Visitors now explore the historic prison on guided audio tours, donning headphones to listen to recorded accounts of its past.[10] They are free to wander through the old cells, step into the infirmary, and view the gallows, all while experiencing a carefully curated and sanitized version of the gaol's harsh reality. No remnants remain of the oppressive conditions once endured – no more days spent sweating in overcrowded cells, sharing a single bucket for a toilet, or sleeping on a mat beside it. The suffocating smells and the pain of confinement have faded into history.

So too has the terror that haunted the ten men who once waited here on death row, anticipating their date with the hangman's noose. Visitors now encounter only the echoes of these stories as they move through the gaol's preserved spaces, safely distanced from the suffering and fear that once defined life behind its walls.

Perhaps as is fitting for murderers, Koci and Novotny and the other executed felons have no marked graves, and their location is officially lost. Nevertheless, and not surprisingly, visitors regularly ask the museum staff where they are buried. It was nearly 75 years ago, but Leo Izod, who was 18 years old at the time, says he remembers graves under the infirmary wall plaques that hold their initials and the date of their executions. In Adelaide Gaol the executed were buried between the gaol walls with the date and their initials placed on the wall above, so it makes sense that this could happen in Fannie Bay also.

In December 2025 I decided to find out. The Museum and Art Gallery of the Northern Territory (MAGNT) gave permission for us to survey 12 square metres of the ground immediately beneath the plaques using a ground penetrating radar (GPR) owned and operated by Wayne Parslow. Wayne's contribution to finding and counting the graves at the 1830's settlement of Fort Victoria in Port Essington was well known to me, and I was thrilled when he quickly came on board.

I met Wayne at the gaol early on a steamy wet-season morning with museum curator Jared Archibald. Wayne wheeled his machine into position and walked back and forward across the ground. In a remarkably simple and quick process, it was obvious that two rectangular 'disturbances' had been carved into the coffee rock beneath our feet – two graves. An undisturbed wall of rock between them confirms they are separate, rather than one big hole, and interestingly the grave on the right, under the initials J.K., is shallower than the other. Maybe the diggers ran out of time, or their equipment failed.

Figure 42: Wayne Parslow using the Ground Penetrating Radar to identify grave shaped cuttings into the bedrock below, in December 2025.

The GPR did not show any human remains of course, and the digital images do not prove that the graves belong to the two Czechs but, we agreed, it is most likely that this patch of ground in Fannie Bay Gaol is indeed their final resting place.

Endnotes

1. A.G. Strath, Keeper, Darwin Gaol and Labour Prison (in Gilruth 1914).
2. *Advertiser*, 13 April 1934, page 21.
3. The last state to remove the death penalty as a punishment was New South Wales in 1985, but by then it was an anachronism as it had not been used in since 1932 anyway, when John Trevor Kelly was hanged at Long Bay Gaol for the murder of Marjorie Sommerlad.
4. Of the other eight executed murderers, only Flannigan's story appears as a part of the exhibition.
5. Leo Izod, personal communication, August 2025.
6. John Flynn, personal communication, August 2025.
7. *Northern Standard*, 3 June 1932, page 3: Fanny Bay Gaol
8. *Northern Standard*, 8 March 1940, page 14: Appalling Conditions at Fanny Bay Gaol
9. *Herald*, 12 December 1953, page 5: Fanny Bay gaol is "barbaric."
10. I was a part of the 'theatre' of recording the noises of prisoners for the audio tour produced by Johanna Bell and Caddie Brain in 2023 (see https://www.magnt.net.au/audiotours). You can hear me complaining and demanding a "smoke" among the clatter of many other volunteer "prisoners." There was no way the fun we had that Saturday morning reflected the discomfort suffered by 97 years of prisoners in this place.

Appendix
The List of Murder Trials 1884-1913

In 1913, the Minister for External Affairs, Patrick Glynn, asked Justice Bevan to collate from the records a list of all murder and manslaughter trials to have taken place in the Northern Territory since settlement. Bevin's list begins in 1884, because prior to that the Northern Territory Courts were not permitted to run murder trials (this is why Wandy Wandy, for instance, was tried for manslaughter in 1879, rather than murder.)

Most trials did not lead to a capital punishment, but the list compiled by Bevan is interesting enough to include here, with those executed identified in bold text.[1]

> List of Murders committed in the Northern Territory, the perpetrators of which were brought to trial, since May 1884.
>
> 1. September 7th, 1884. Houschildt, Schollert, Noltenius and Landers murdered at Daly River copper mine; several natives were convicted and sentenced to death; the sentence was commuted to imprisonment for life.
>
> 2. September 21st. 1884. R. v Ah Kong, for murder of James Lawless; guilty. Verdict set aside by full court in Adelaide. In December 1885 Ah Kong was again put on his trial and found guilty and sentenced to death, but the conviction was again upset by the full court. Cf. S.A.L.R. vol. XX p.65.
>
> 3. December 1884. Alleged murder of a chinaman [sic] by a

---

[1]   NAA, A3 NT1914/426.

fellow countryman at McKinley River. Not guilty.

4. April 1885. R. v Candalamah, for murder of Ah Foo. Guilty; sentence commuted to imprisonment for life.

5. February 1886. R. v Tommy Dodd: for murder of black boy named Palmer; guilty.

6. August 1886. R. v Heath; for murder of McKinnon; guilty of manslaughter.

7. March 1886. R. v Whitton, for murder of Thomas Spellicy and Ah Young. Guilty. Before execution, the condemned man became insane and was removed to Adelaide. Cf. S.A.L.R. Vol. XXI.

8. November 1888. R. v Anderson, for murder of Walter Daniel Hammond; guilty of manslaughter.

9. April 1889. R. v Spencer for murder of a native; guilty. A most deliberate murder: the accused shot the man through the head while two of his boys held him, calmly saying "Goodbye" as he shot him. The jury added a recommendation to mercy, on what ground it is quite impossible to see from the report of the case. The sentence was commuted to imprisonment for life, and after a short term the murderer was released on petition, but some years later was killed by natives and his camp looted.

10. June 1893. R. v Long and Kearney, for the murder of a chinaman at Middle Springs; verdict Not Guilty. The jury returned their verdict without hearing the defence. This case caused considerable stir in Adelaide (see files of The Register about August 25th. 1892) and it was suggested in Parliament that trial by jury in the Northern Territory should be abolished.

11. September 1892. R. v Flannigan (half caste) for murder of S. Croker; guilty; execution carried out at Darwin [Hanged in Fannie Bay Gaol on 15 July 1893].

12. October 1892. R. v Wanchill and Warrima, aboriginal natives for the murder of Ah Kim; Warrima found guilty of murder, and Wanchill guilty of manslaughter.

13. May 1892. R. v 8 natives for the murder of 6 Malays, Guilty. The sentences of 7 were commuted to imprisonment for life and one, Wandy Wandy, was

executed at the scene of the murder [Hanged at Malay Bay on 25 July 1893].

14. **June 1894. R. v Nyanko and Moolooloorun, for the murder of a Chinaman; Guilty; the sentence of one was commuted to imprisonment for life; the other was executed near where the crime took place** [Moolooloorun was hanged at Mole Hill on 17 January 1895].

15. April 1898. R. v Okomoto for murder of a Japanese Diver; Jury disagreed, and the prisoner pleaded guilty to manslaughter.

16. January 1896. R. v Charley for the murder of two Chinamen; hot guilty.

17. December 1896. R. v Carrara and Peter2, for the murder of T. A. Perry; Carrara not guilty, Peter guilty.

18. November 1897. R. v Ryland for murder of McDonald; jury failed to agree, and the crown accepted a plea of guilty of manslaughter.

19. April 1898. R. v Okomoto. See above; no. 15.

20. **July 1898. R. v Lem Kai and Chung Leung [Yeung] for murder of fellow countryman; guilty; executed at Darwin** [Hanged in Fannie Bay Gaol on 10 August 1899].

21. December 1898. R. v Narbaloora and Copperang for the murder of Moore and Mackenzie; guilty; sentence commuted to imprisonment for life and the prisoners were discharged after serving a short time as the motive for the crime was to rescue two lubras who had been forcibly removed from their country.

22. A Malay was convicted of murder of a fellow countryman and sentenced to death, but the sentence was commuted to imprisonment for life.

23 July 1900. A Chinaman was tried for the murder of two natives by poison and found not guilty.

24. **July 1900. A native was convicted and executed on the Victoria River for the murder of one John Larsen** ["Jimmy," hanged at Shaws Creek on 8 April 1901].

25. June 1902. R. v Ashton for the murder of Ah Lip at Yam Creek: not guilty. A most brutal case, the jury after retiring for half an hour, returned and asked, "can the jury find

being an accessory to manslaughter?" His Honour "Upon the facts of the case you cannot find the prisoner guilty of manslaughter as an accessory before the fact. The evidence given for the prisoner goes to show that he was the aider and abettor of a blackfellow in killing this man, and if you believe that, he is just as guilty in the eye of the law as the man who actually did the deed. I have already explained to you the distinction between murder and manslaughter. If you find that the prisoner was present aiding and abetting, it lies with you to return a verdict of either murder or manslaughter". The Foreman. "In that case, your Honour, the verdict is not guilty."

26. **January 1905. R. v Tommy for the murder of H. Edwards, R. Frost and, a native woman at Spring Creek Victoria River. Guilty; executed in Darwin gaol** ["Alligator River Tommy" hanged in Fannie Bay Gaol on 21 December 1905].

27. May 1905. R. v an aboriginal native for the murder of James Mildwater Guilty with a strong recommendation to mercy; the sentence was commuted to imprisonment for life. In this case the murdered man took the accused's lubra, tying her up in his camp, and on the accused remonstrating the murdered man fired at him with a gun which missed the accused who then killed his assailant.

28. June 1906. R. v Nolan and Turner for the murder of Charlie and Port Darwin Jack, aboriginal natives. Not guilty. In this case the evidence of the actual killing was sworn to by three eyewitnesses, natives, whose testimony was unshaken and uncontradicted. Circumstantial evidence of the strongest kind was given; the finding of human bones in the fire at the accused's camp; blood stains where the killing was alleged to have taken place; the finding of a Browning pistol bullet in the remains that fitted the Browning pistol in the possession of one of the accused, and this evidence was in no way discredited or contradicted. No evidence was called for the accused save as to character. The main point in the defence was the absence of motive, the accused according to the evidence of the eyewitnesses, having calmly shot down the natives after they, the natives, had refused to go away with the accused. It is interesting to quote a passage from the report of the case in

the *Northern Territory Times* of August 3rd, 1906. "The finding of the jury came as a surprise to many, the general impression being that there would probably be a disagreement".

29 November 1905. R. v Cumbitt and Donah for the murder of Bradshaw, Skeehan, Dannock and Eggoriffe [sic: Eggeroff]; Guilty; sentence commuted to life imprisonment. There was a recommendation to mercy on the ground of provocation through the ill treatment of the natives by Egoriffe [sic].

30 October 1906. R. v Ben, a South Sea Islander for the murder of a fellow country man; guilty of manslaughter.

31. January 1907. R. v Nim Sam and Robert for the murder of a blackfellow named Peter. Guilty of manslaughter. This was a case in which the accused stole the kidney fat of the murdered man for medicine purposes.

32. March 1908. R. v Dick and Charlie for the murder of Chong Ling. verdict, Dick not guilty, Charlie Guilty; sentence commuted to life imprisonment.

33. May 1908. R. v Frank, an aboriginal native for the murder of a native named Pierre, Plea of guilty of manslaughter accepted.

34. October 1908. R. v Hume and Paddy Bull (a half caste native) for the murder of a native. Hume not guilty, Paddy Bull guilty; the sentence was commuted to imprisonment for life. To quote from the Northern Territory Times of April 30th, 1909. "The announcement of the verdict was received silently, and we believe it came as somewhat of a surprise to the majority of those present".

35. February 1909. R. v Willie, an aboriginal for the murder of a fellow tribesman; not guilty.

36. April 1909. R. v Pupelee and aboriginal for murder of Thomas Egan; Guilty, commuted to imprisonment for life. The crime was provoked through the deceased interfering with the accused's lubra.

37. May 1909. R. v Cumberwell an aboriginal, for the murder of a lubra guilty of manslaughter.

38. January 1910. Two natives were convicted of the murder of a white man named Ward. The sentence was commuted to imprisonment for life.

39. January 1911. R. v Smith for the murder of a native named Frank; not guilty.

As to the cases that have occurred since my appointment to the position of Judge of the Northern Territory, full notes of these are already in the hands of the Minister, or of the Department of External Affairs.

Signed by Justice Bevan 3/12/1913.

Bibliography

Berry, J. (1892). *My Experiences as an Executioner*. Accessed 25/08/2025: www.gutenberg.org/files/46579.

Buchanan, G. (1933). *Packhorse and Waterhole*. Angus and Robertson.

Buchanan, R. (1997). *In the Tracks of Old Bluey*. Brisbane: Queensland University Press.

Christopherson, D. (2023). *A Little Bit of Justice*. Darwin: CDU Press.

Creaghe, E. C. (1883). *The Diary of Emily Caroline Creaghe: Explorer*. Edited with Introduction by Peter Monteath: Corkwood Press, 2004.

Dewar, M. (1999). *Inside Out*. Darwin: NTU Press.

Donovan, P. (1981). *The Northern Territory: A History of South Australia's Northern Territory*. St. Lucia: University of Queensland.

Elder, P. (2008). Kriewaldt, (Rudolf) Martin Chemnitz (1900-1960). In Carment, *N.T. Dictionary of Biography, Revised Edition* (p. 328). Darwin: Charles Darwin University Press (on line).

Farrer, V. (2014). *Ellen Thomson: Beyond a Reasonable Doubt?* ACT: Halstead Press.

Gaunt, C. (1931-1934, A serialised memoir). Old Time Memories. *Northern Standard*.

Gilruth, J. (1914). *Report of the Administrator for the Year 1913*. Darwin: Parliament of the Commonwealth of Australia.

Hodge, B. (2005). *Walk On: The remarkable true story of the last person sentenced to death in Australia*. Perth: Rowville: The Five Mile Press.

Johns, J. (1913). *Katterinyah, Murder, July 14th, 1913, Evidence*. NT1913-11019. National Archives of Australia, NT1913-11019.

Jones, T. (1990). *The Chinese in the Northern Territory*. Darwin: NTU Press.

Kimber, R. G. (1990). *Stott, Robert (1858–1928), Australian Dictionary of Biography, Australian National University*. Retrieved April 18, 2021, from https://adb.anu.edu.au/biography/stott-robert-8690/text15203

Kriewaldt, M. (1952). *Judgements of the Supreme Court of the Northern Territory of Australia, p 145 – 155*. Darwin: Northern Territory Government.

Lewis, D. (1998). Patrolling the 'Big Up': the Adventures of Mounted Constable Johns in the Top End of the Northern Territory 1910-1915. Darwin: Historical Society of the Northern Territory.

Lewis, D. (2004). A Wild History: life and death on the Victoria River frontier. Melbourne: Monash University Press.

Lewis, D. (2022, December 9). Victoria River District Doomsday Book. Retrieved from https://doi.org/10.31235/osf.io/kfmnz: https://doi.org/10.31235/osf.io/kfmnz

Little, J. (11 August 1993). The Hanging of Wandy Wandy. Palmerston: Northern Territory Times and Gazette.

Norcock, G. (1895). Gaol and Labour Prison: Government Resident's Report. Adelaide, p12.: South Australian Government.

O'Sullivan, V. (2018/003). Hanging Down Under: Capital Punishment and Deterrence in Australia. Lancaster University Management School: Economics Working Paper Series.

Pugh, D. (2021). Darwin: Growth of a City: The 1880s. Darwin: www.derekpugh.com.au.

Pugh, D. (2022). Twenty to the Mile: The Overland Telegraph Line. Darwin: www.derekpugh.com.au.

Pugh, D. (2023). Darwin: Survival of a City, The 1890s. Darwin: www.derekpugh.com.au.

Pugh, D. (2024). The Ragged Thirteen: Territory Bushrangers. Darwin: www.derekpugh.com.au.

Pugh, D. (2025). Darwin, End of an Era, 1900-1911. Darwin: www.derekpugh.com.au.

Reid, G. (1990). A picnic with the Natives: Aboriginal-European Relations in the Northern Territory to 1910. Melbourne: Melbourne University Press.

Roberts, T. (2005). Frontier Justice: a History of the Gulf Country to 1900. Brisbane: University of Queensland Press.

Roberts, T. (2009, September 14). The Brutal Truth: What happened in the Gulf Country. Retrieved from The Monthly: https://www.themonthly.com.au/issue/2009/november/

Rogers, J. (2014). When Islam came to Australia. Retrieved 16 September 2025: BBC News.

Ryan, L., & Pascoe, W. (2019). Colonial Frontier Massacres. Retrieved from University of Newcastle, Centre for 21st Century Humanities: https://c21ch.newcastle.edu.au/colonialmassacres/detail.php?r=704

Searcy, A. (1905). In Northern Seas: being Mr. Alfred Searcy's experiences on the north coast of Australia by Searcy, Alfred, 1854-1925, as recounted to Whitington, E. (Ernest), 1873-1934. digitised version.

Searcy, A. (1909). *In Australian Tropics.* London: G. Robertson.

Smith, R. (2024). *Licence to Kill: Massacre Men in Australia's North.* Darwin: Historical Society of the Northern Territory.

Wade, S. (2009). *Britain's Most Notorious Hangmen.* London: Wharncliffe Books.

Index

Symbols
13-Mile 100

A
Adelaide Gaol 16, 118, 146
Adelaide River 83, 110
Ah Lin 78
Ah Loy 90, 92
Ah Wah, Joe 5, 6, 11
Angalarri River (Shaws Creek) 65
Angareeda 24, 26, 27

anti-Chinese feelings 35
Anyuana 80, 81, 83, 84, 88, 89, 90, 94
Archibald, Jared iii, xvii, 146
Armstrong's Farm 73
Arnhem Land xviii, 22
Arramboon 24, 25
Auvergne Station 1, 5, 6, 14

B
Banka Banka 110
Barbier 121
Barney 6, 11
Batten, William 43
Benamulla 74
Benning, Henry "Dutchy" 69
Berry, James 133, 136
Bevan, Justice David xxi, xxii, 85, 86, 87, 89, 92, 93, 95, 96, 149, 154
Billy, a tracker 40

black boys 22
Black Maria 113
Bradshaw, Joe 55
Bradshaw's Run 65
Brocks Creek 77, 80, 82, 83
Brocks Creek Police Station 78
Brophie, Sergeant 7, 10
Buchanan, Gordon 2
Buchanan, Nat 'Bluey' 2
Burrundie 46, 47, 77

C
Cahill, Paddy 85, 86
Cameron, Mounted Constable Harry 94
Campbell, Duncan 3
Capoondur xviii, 24, 25, 26, 29
Carey, Government Secretary Henry 86, 95
Chee Hang ix, 47, 48, 77
Chinese people in the Territory 35
Ching Loy ix, 77, 78

Christophersen, Don xxiii
Chung Yeung ix, 47, 48, 49, 52
Circuit Court 14, 19, 27, 33, 40, 42, 46, 50, 54, 61, 63, 67
Clayton, David 108
Cockatoo 62
Cosmo-Howley Mine 77
Crawford, Lindsay 4
Creagh, Emily 4

Crescent Lagoon ix, 37, 38, 42, 43, 44
Criminal Law Consolidation Act 65

D

Daly River 55, 56, 57, 58, 62, 65, 67, 80, 81, 94, 95, 149
Daly Waters 104, 106, 128
Darwin Taxi-owners' Association 98
Dashwood, Justice Charles xvii, xxiii, 14, 40, 41, 61
De Latour, George 43

Croker, Samuel Burns 2
Cusack, Tom 70

Diana's Diary 97, 98, 128
Don Hotel 108, 110
Dooramite 24
Duchess 101, 102, 110
Dunleavy, Magistrate 102

E

Edmunds, Keith 117, 118, 119, 122, 125, 129
Edwards, Henry ix, 69
Egeroff, Ivan 55, 59, 61, 62

Elsey Station 34, 37
Executive Committee 65
Executive Council xix, 29, 41

F

Fannie Bay Gaol ix, xvii, xxii, xxiii, xxv, 15, 21, 41, 47, 69, 72, 74, 75, 97, 113, 118, 122, 127, 142, 144, 145, 150, 152
Fitzmaurice River 81
Flannigan, Charlie ix, xvii, xx, xxii, xxiii, 1, 14, 17

Fletcher, Reverend D. 75
Foelsche, Inspector Paul 11, 30
Freer, Cecil 70
Frost, Richard ix, 69

G

Gardens Hill Cemetery 141
Gee Chong Foong 63
Gilruth, John xxi
Glynn, Minister Patrick xxii, 85, 86, 87, 149
Goolarguo xviii, 29
Grantham, Dulcie 97, 101, 141

Grantham, George Thomas 97, 99, 141
Griffiths, Walter xix
Ground Penetrating Radar 146
Gunn, Jeanie 18
Gurindji 4

H

Halls Creek 7, 10
Hatton, Constable Herbert 101
Herbert, Charles xx, 49

Hodge, Brenda xxii
Hollow, Constable Tom 102
Hughes, Attorney General W.M. 87

I

Ingeewaraky 24
Iwaidja 21, 22, 30

Izod, Leo 124, 141

J

Jan, Novotny 97
Jessop, Keith 98

Jessop's Taxis 98
Jimmy 55, 59

Johns, Mounted Constable John (Jack) 78, 80, 82, 88

K
Katherine 2, 18, 36, 46, 98, 128
Katherine River 5
Katterinyan 80, 81, 83, 84, 89, 90, 91, 92, 93, 94, 95
Kelly, Mortimer 7
Kelly, Mounted Constable James 70

L
Larry, tracker 83
Larson, John ix, 55, 61, 65
Lem Kai 47, 49, 52
Little, Egbert Percy Graham 63

M
MacKillop, Father Donald 22
Makassans 22, 23
Malay Bay ix, xviii, 21, 23, 30, 151
Mandool 23, 24, 26, 27
Mangerippy 24, 31
Mangulmangul xxii
Mankee xxii
Marragin xxii
Marwood, William 132, 133
Mataranka 43
Mattacajaiah 91
Mayuna 21
McArthur River Police Station 36
McDougall, Herbert 100
McFarland, Senior Constable Lionel 111
McKell, Sir William John 117
McManus, Charlie 1
McNab, Sergeant Eric 102, 106

N
Napoo 81
Nargoon xxii
Negri Station 7, 10
Neimann, Harry 56

Johnston, Charles 43
Johnston, Frank 111

Kirkland, Charles xx
Koci, Jaroslav 97, 99, 106, 117
Kolbung 90
Koppio 80, 84, 87
Kriewaldt, Justice Martin xxiii, 107, 108, 113

Little, John Archibald Graham xvii, 30, 44, 52, 136
Lockwood, Douglas 144
Long Peter 63
Lo Sin ix, 77, 78, 91

McPhee, Jock 5, 6, 8, 9, 12, 18
Millikan, Reverend W. A. xviii
Minemarra xxii
Minniehaha 55, 56, 57, 62
Mintaedge xviii, 24, 25, 26, 27, 29
Mitchell, Samuel xx
Mole Hill ix, 33, 38, 40, 44, 45, 151
Moolooloorun ix, 33, 37, 38, 39, 40, 41, 42, 44, 45, 65, 151
Mount Isa 103, 110
Mr. "Smith", hangman 121
Mugg, Captain 55, 56, 62, 67
Murphy, Bernard 2
Murray, Robert 6
Museum and Art Gallery of the Northern Territory 146
Mutch, Sergeant Verdon 100, 102, 104, 106, 110, 111

Nemarluk xxii
Newcastle Waters 3
Newell, A. B. 110, 111
Norcock, George 16, 51, 117, 129

Northern Territory Justice Act xx
Novotny, Jan 99, 108, 117

O

Odlum J.P., R. L. 122
Oenpelli 94
O'Flaherty, Doctor 34, 41

P

Paddy Disher, tracker 83
Page, Charles xviii

R

Rapid Creek Mission 22
Robinson, E. O. 21, 22, 26, 28
Roper River Police Station 33, 35

S

Schombacher, Mrs Georgina 108
Scott, Mounted Constable Robert 33
Scott, Sid 4
Searcy, Alfred 22, 23, 31, 46
Shaws Creek ix, 55, 151
Shierlaw, Defence Counsel H. A. 139
Sportsmans Arms and General Store 2
Spriggs, a gaol guard 94
Stichling, George 63

T

The Fannie Bay Gaol 142
The Gardens Cemetery 141
Thomas Andrea 65, 66
Timber Creek 5

V

Victoria River 3, 56, 57, 65, 67, 69, 71, 84, 151, 152

W

Wandy Wandy ix, xviii, xix, xx, xxii, 21, 22, 23, 24, 25, 26, 29, 31, 43, 150
Waters, N 27
Watson, Jack 'The Gulf Hero' 4
Wave Hill Station 3, 5, 7
Wingfield, Howard 21, 22

Nowra ix, 69
Nyanko 38, 39

Old Howley Mine ix
Ord River Station 7

Parslow, Wayne 146
Pine Creek 4, 35, 38, 44, 48, 63, 77, 79, 98

Ryan, Ronald x, 140
Ryland, George 51

Stone, Mounted Constable Fred 58
Stott, Mounted Constable Robert 35, 45, 46, 58
Strath, Warden A. G. 72, 139
Stretton, Mounted Constable 36
Stretton, William xxi, 85, 92
Sugarbag 94
Supreme Court of the Northern Territory xxi, 117

Tommy, Alligator River ix, 69, 72, 74, 152
Tommy, tracker 83
Travers, Bill 3

Victoria River Station 59

Wise, Administrator Frank 115
Wolgera 94
Woods, Mounted Constable 94
Wunwulla 55, 67
Würgegalgen 131
Wyndham 10

Y

Yam Creek ix, 47, 50, 54, 77, 151

Further readings

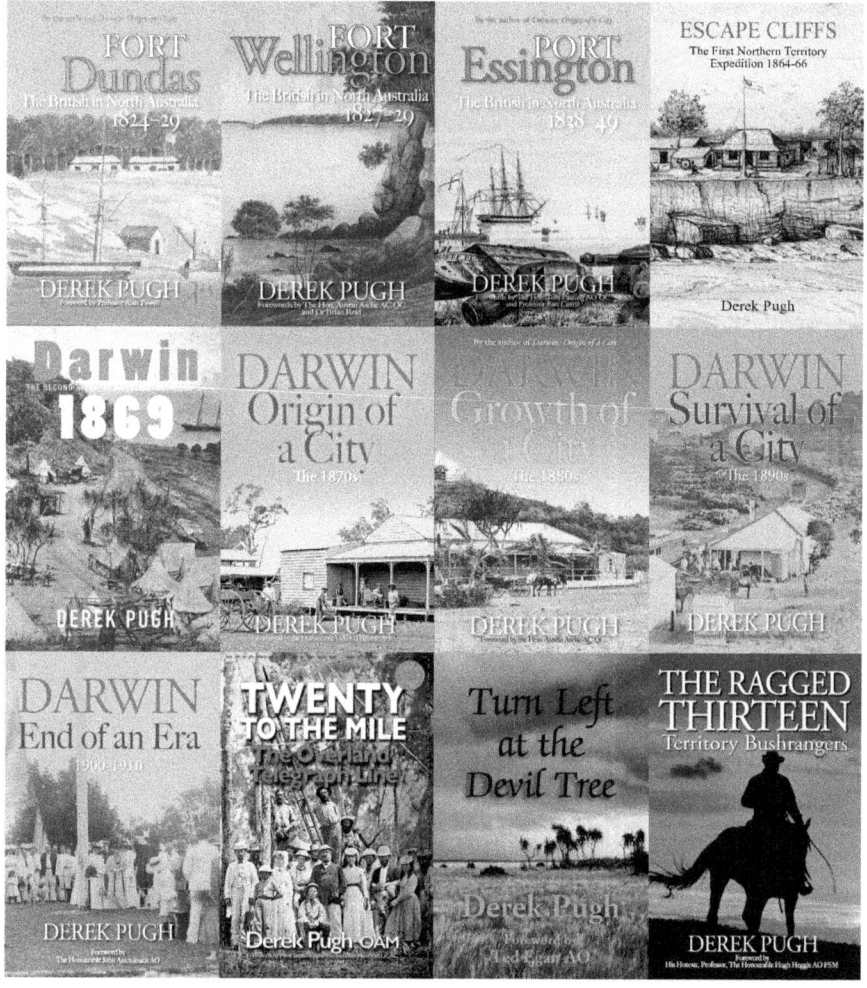

www.derekpugh.com.au

www.ingramcontent.com/pod-product-compliance
Lightning Source LLC
Chambersburg PA
CBHW060836170426
43192CB00019BA/2797